SANSHÔ DAYÛ

山椒太夫

· · · · · · · · · · · · · · · · · ·

Dudley Andrew & Carole Cavanaugh

bfi Publishing

First published in 2000 by the
BRITISH FILM INSTITUTE
21 Stephen Street, London W1P 2LN

The British Film Institute
promotes greater understanding
and appreciation of, and
access to, film and moving image
culture in the UK.

British Library Cataloguing-in-Publication Data
A catalogue record for this book is available from the British Library

ISBN 0–85170–541–3

Series design by
Andrew Barron & Collis Clements Associates

Typeset in Fournier and Franklin Gothic by
D R Bungay Associates, Burghfield, Berks

Printed in Great Britain by The Cromwell Press, Trowbridge, Wiltshire

CONTENTS

. . . .

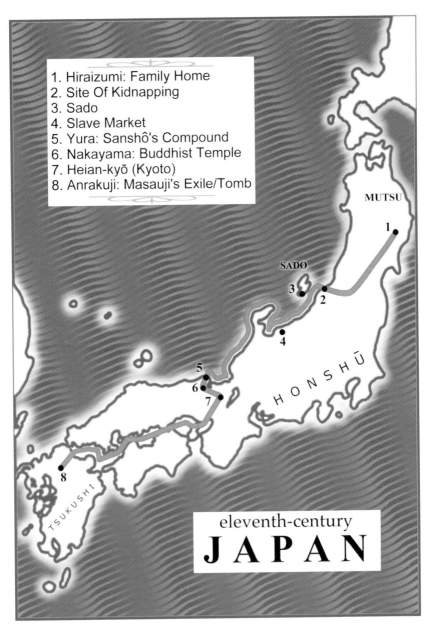

1. Hiraizumi: Family Home
2. Site Of Kidnapping
3. Sado
4. Slave Market
5. Yura: Sanshô's Compound
6. Nakayama: Buddhist Temple
7. Heian-kyō (Kyoto)
8. Anrakuji: Masauji's Exile/Tomb

MUTSU

SADO

HONSHŪ

TSUKUSHI

eleventh-century
JAPAN

(Map adapted from various sources by Christopher Miller)

PREFACE

....

Sanshô Dayû was tossed like a stone into the cultural pool of the Venice film festival in 1954. The expanding circles of its impact would over the years be amplified by other circles sent out after its 1960 Paris release (where it topped *Cahiers du Cinéma*'s annual list) and then after its appearance in the United States in 1968. Both of us watched it reverentially in the auteurist aura of those times, and felt it plunge into our lives. Separately, haphazardly, we read and talked about it, each developing a private conversation about a private *Sanshô*. But conversations are never really one's own, though they may carry a personal tone. Dudley Andrew, for his part, put *Sanshô* in dialogue with other Mizoguchi films he actively sought out, and with both the history of film style and the European aesthetic concepts that have long governed his experiences of films. For Carole Cavanaugh, the film opened a dialogue between Japanese film and literature and across two eras, Heian and Taishô – lush times separated by a thousand years but in touch with each other in their desire to link the verbal and the visual. When eventually we met, these distinct discursive waves came into contact and mounted in amplitude, figuring new patterns and unexpected arabesques, worth fixing in this book, if only as another disturbance in the cultural eddy Mizoguchi put in motion with his film forty-five years ago.

We are glad that one of us is female, the other male; that one of us is a student of Japanese culture, the other of European; that one is devoted to the study of words and pictures, and the other to cinematic style. When superimposed, these backgrounds display in relief the sterling film that stands foregrounded even by the disparity of our views. Cavanaugh, recognising Mizoguchi's late rejection of the ideology that devastated Asia and enslaved Japan, finds *Sanshô Dayû* to be a renunciation of the militarist misuse of Japanese philosophical traditions. Andrew, attuned to the post-war European discourse of humanism, takes *Sanshô* to uphold tradition, indeed to assert a Japanese origin to the democratic values imposed on the nation by the United States. Listening to conversations inside and outside Japan respectively, we put our views here in conversation with each other, for our subject is the same: namely Mizoguchi's anxiety in the face of modernity. In different ways we each position his retelling of a beloved tale in anything but a comfortable space.

We are elated that our chapters, styled independently, seem resonant when read together. For this is how we worked: writing entirely on our own, then each enhancing our chapters after engaging with what the other had written. And so this book does not set out to render a single argument, nor does it represent a division of labour. It renders, rather, a conversation (in the full sense Stanley Cavell gives that term) around something very worth talking about: a powerful film and its varied experience in ourselves and in the cultures we, in our distinctive keys, cannot help but echo. Andrew believes that Mizoguchi sublimates a folk tradition into an art film that has participated in the global discourse of post-war humanism and that has entered a world community of cinephiles inhabited by the likes of Jean-Luc Godard and Terrence Malick. Cavanaugh is less concerned with the exoteric authority of Western discourse than with the timeless attachments of faith and family, passionate bonds at the heart of a story supple enough to withstand a millennium of political and societal change. The fact that these interpretations do not come harmoniously into phase demonstrates once again that profound works of art leave their futures open to unforeseeable and conflicting understandings. This does not mean that artworks are awash in a sea of interpretation. *Sanshô Dayû* resolutely, implacably guides both our readings; it is the source of our divagations. Indeed, in its generosity *Sanshô Dayû* activates a surplus of meaning beyond us, beyond even itself.

SYNOPSIS

An aristocratic family threads its way through a forest in eleventh-century Japan. The mother Tamaki, her daughter Anju, and her son Zushiô recall the family trauma that has dislodged them from their manor in the northeast of Honshû. Seven years earlier the father of the family, Taira no Masauji, governor of the area, was dishonoured and exiled for supporting human rights. As he was taken away, he passed the family heirloom, a small statue of the Bodhisattva deity Kannon, to his son with the exhortation 'A man without compassion is no longer human....' Zushiô now repeats the maxim to his mother Tamaki, encouraging her in their journey. When they are forced to camp in an especially forlorn grove, not far from the Japan Sea, a supposed Shinto priestess takes them in, only to betray them in the morning to pirates. The nurse is drowned; the mother is kidnapped to the island of Sado, while her children are bound over to the notorious Sanshô, who enslaves them in a huge labour compound on the mainland coast far west of Sado. Sanshô's cruel methods are productive, making him the local minister's favourite vassal; nevertheless, his own son Tarô so abhors the slave-camp that, upon hearing the sad history of these delicate children, he runs away to a nearby Buddhist temple protected by state authority.

Ten years pass. Zushiô has given up his principles and become one of Sanshô's overseers. He even cruelly brands a runaway, shocking the still faithful Anju. One day Anju hears a new slave-girl sing, 'Zushiô, Anju, where are you?' – a doleful tune an old prostitute named Nakagimi was known to wail on the island of Sado. As Anju showers the bewildered girl with questions she cannot answer, a cut to Sado shows us that Tamaki is indeed Nakagimi; we see her attempt to escape by boat. She is caught, maimed and left to hobble to a lookout to sing her song into the wind and across the sea to the mainland.

Even this indirect news that their mother may be alive fails to affect the hardened Zushiô. On orders from Sanshô, he icily prepares to abandon Anju's dying friend Namiji in the forest. Anju, who has been given permission to accompany her brother on this burial mission, insists that they construct a makeshift shelter for her friend's final resting place. Scavenging for wood, the siblings hang on a branch until they break it and tumble together. Both instantly recall the last night they had spent with their mother, when in building the forest shelter they had tumbled together in precisely this way. The mother's cry 'Zushiô, Anju' wafts its way to them mysteriously from Sado or from out of the past, and Zushiô melts in contrition. Determined to flee together, Zushiô grabs the old slave Namiji, but Anju demurs, saying that someone must delay the guards. They tearfully part. Zushiô seeks safety in the mountain temple presided over by none other than Sanshô's son Tarô; Anju decoys the guards as long as possible and then slips serenely into a forest pond, where she can escape Sanshô's tortures and hope to find in death the spirit of her father.

Secretly reaching the court at Kyoto, Zushiô throws himself at the feet of the premier. He is rebuffed, even imprisoned, until the premier recognises his family heirloom and raises him to honour. It seems that the regime that deposed his father has in the meantime fallen, and although the father recently died in exile, the new premier can console Zushiô by awarding him the governorship of Tango, the province containing Sanshô's compound.

Against all advice, and without real jurisdiction, Zushiô's first act as governor is to free all slaves in his province. The astounded Sanshô is exiled, and his camp is burned by revelling slaves. Disheartened to learn of Anju's suicide and certain of the legal reprisals about to bear down on him, Zushiô immediately resigns his position and journeys as a free man to Sado, seeking his mother.

He looks in vain in the brothels but gets word that an old woman named Nakagimi may be living in a hut by the sea. On a craggy, desolate shore Zushiô asks a seaweed gatherer for directions. Further on he finds a blind old woman, his mother, sitting alone in the sand by her miserable hut. At first she refuses to believe it is Zushiô, so often have the islanders teased her about her lament. But upon touching the heirloom and hearing him recall her husband's sacred bequest, she falls into Zushiô's arms. They mourn the dissolution of their family in exile and death, as the camera cranes away from them, framing the coastline where the lone seaweed gatherer goes about his inexorable labour.

'SANSHÔ DAYÛ' AND THE OVERTHROW OF HISTORY

. . . .

Carole Cavanaugh

The thousand-year-old legend of the enslavement of Anju and Zushiô, the story made familiar by Mori Ôgai's 1915 narrative and Mizoguchi's 1954 film *Sanshô Dayû* (*Sanshô the Bailiff*), is remarkable not only for its long career but for its resilience over centuries of revisions and retellings. Every version originates with political exile, so it seems natural that politics has used the story for its own purposes.[1] But as useful as public discourse has found the tale, it is not the conflicting interactions of men and governments in the narrative that have kept the story alive. Societal concerns diminish before the consecrating authority of family affection, a force in the end untouched by politics, and all the more sustaining for its innocence. The tale endures despite the transformations in plot and pace demanded by ideology, because in every rendition the narrative retains a tenacious imagination of the family and its powerful attachments.

Sanshô Dayû is a romance of separation and the desire for return, a desire that has drawn the legend into retellings in two styles in the twentieth century, one traditional and one modern, because both of these, the fairy-tale and the melodrama, share a preoccupation with the

Illustration of kidnapping in a seventeenth-century text

life-transitions of individuals in their roles as members of families. The fairy-tale fixation on the achievements of the child structures the Ôgai version; the melodrama's intense concern with adult children in disrupted families underpins Mizoguchi's film. The choice of style is not arbitrary; each teller of the Sanshô tale responds to the pressures of his historical moment, and so any notion that either the fairy-tale or melodrama trivialises its content must be abandoned. The difference in their views of history accounts not only for the sharp contrast between Ôgai and Mizoguchi in their political interpretations, but also for the narrative modes that express those positions.

An awareness of the ideological interaction between Ôgai and Mizoguchi gives access to the cultural context within which Japanese audiences may have understood the film when it was released not quite a decade after the end of the Pacific War. Ôgai, who died in 1922, remained a renowned intellectual who actively participated in the modernisation project of the late nineteenth century but later questioned its validity. Mizoguchi was a child of the new century, an artist in an imported medium, a contemporary whose generation had lived through national devastation previously unimaginable. Perhaps the only similarity between the two men is that both came to the Sanshô legend in their fifties, late in their careers and after they had experienced profound changes in their political views. For Ôgai, history had become a new site of wisdom, a place of certainty and moral closure. For Mizoguchi, history had diverged irrevocably from tradition and had turned into a darkening shroud from which we struggle unsuccessfully to emerge.

The Sanshô Legend as Confucian Politics

It is safe to say that Mizoguchi would not have retold the Sanshô story in film if Mori Ôgai (1862–1922) had not recaptured the legend in contemporary prose. The director did not recover a tale from ancient times but retold a classic well known and widely read by his viewers in school textbooks. Just as Akutagawa Ryûnsuke (1892–1927) stood as early-century *accoucheur* between the thirteenth-century *Konjaku monogatari* and Kurosawa's *Rashômon* (1950), Ôgai mediated for Mizoguchi between the medieval and the modern. The political parallels between 1915 and 1954 are striking; in both eras a liberalised Japan was moving away from traditional systems with a rapidity that spurred art briefly but significantly to revisit the past. Whatever its motivations, the return to classical sources in the early twentieth century was more than nostalgic; literature was captivated by its ability to reinvent itself through a combination of naive content with sophisticated narrative technique. Historical fiction arose in reaction to Naturalism, a Japanese literary movement very different from its European namesake. Naturalism in Japan emphasised not social realism but the creation of the Subject through personal observation and an absence of critique. The result was an enervating impressionism. Ôgai's achievement was to remove the Subject but to keep the naturalist style. He claimed that he was applying to history the techniques of observation that Naturalism had developed for the 'I-novel' (*watakushi shôsetsu*). 'If contemporary authors can write about life "just as it is" and find it satisfactory,' he explained, 'then they ought to appreciate a similar treatment of the past.'[2] His relocation of fiction unexpectedly authorised a kind of scientific objectivity that was new to Japanese writing and at the same time had the effect of transporting literature away from the alienating and ultimately irresolvable conflicts of modernity.

But Ôgai's attraction to the remote past was more than a reaction to social transition; it was a philosophical exploration of behaviour within an ethical system that his narratives proposed for recovery in the present. Most of his works in this phase are about men and their families in the late Tokugawa (1603–1867) or early Meiji (1868–1911) periods, who are called upon to act according to Confucian ethics or samurai values. It has been said that no sword is as sharp as Ôgai's pen. A military surgeon himself, his unromanticised retellings of combat and ritual suicide leave no doubt that the samurai blade cut the belly brutally deep. His greater accomplishment, at a time when other writers of his stature imagined only disaffected intellectuals as their protagonists, was to sense how profoundly the values that inspired his samurai heroes incised the modern psyche. We must remind ourselves that by 1915 Japan had moved far away from its samurai past; Ôgai was writing in the most liberal period in Japanese history, well before militarism had fully gripped the nation and only at the beginning of Japan's imperialist enterprise. But he was ahead of his times. His *rekishi monogatari*, the historical-fiction genre he invented in 1912 with 'The Death Note of Okitsu Yagoemon', heralds the resurrection of military ethics as a viable national system fifteen years before the Manchurian Incident. 'Sanshô Dayû' is no doubt the most beloved of these historical works.

Ôgai's political views are consonant with his service as an army medical officer in Japan's emerging colonialist ventures in Taiwan and Manchuria. The same fusion of neo-Confucianism with nationalism that provided the philosophical basis for Japanese imperialism animates his *rekishi monogatari*. His version of 'Sanshô Dayû' is fascinated by Imperial rule, a power interpreted by neo-Confucianism to legitimise Japanese encroachment in other parts of Asia. Ôgai's reconstruction of history as modern fiction prefigures the 1930s nationalist attempt to reconstruct modern Japan on the framework of a neo-Confucian past, through an ideology that sought to maintain the status quo of hierarchical rule in opposition to foreign liberalising forces. It should be noted here that the anti-militarism of Mizoguchi's film is nowhere in evidence in the 1915 story.

Ôgai's renowned detachment is all the more apparent in his dispassionate treatment of the Sanshô legend. The poignancy of the family's plight speaks more eloquently than the author's spare style, and this complexity is of course a mark of Ôgai's genius. But in answer to his acclaimed 'objectivity' and to his self-claimed 'reverence for reality'[3] this

chapter makes the counter-claim that Ôgai spurns realism. Instead, he reworks his historical source material[4] into the unrealistic structure of the fairy-tale to reinforce its reassuring ideological purposes, an interpretation that pretends that slavery is not savage, that exploitation leaves no scars, and that rectification of hierarchy heals all social wounds.

Visible and intriguing stylistic elements own up to the narrative's fairy-tale structure, and the most prominent is Ôgai's happy ending.[5] The family has suffered the loss of both father and sister, but Zushiô is politically reinstated and finds his blind mother, who can now rejoin her son to resume their aristocratic life. No similar sense of resolution attends the film. Other fairy-tale features precede this resolution. Each child – not just Zushiô – carries an important possession. Anju's is an amulet of Jizô – a symbol of spirituality and the efficacy of religious belief; Zushiô's is a sword he has been given by his father – a symbol of the boy's inalienable connection to patriarchal authority. The experiences of both brother and sister during their enslavement are conspicuously parallel: both are given difficult but manageable tasks to perform – he to collect three bundles of firewood a day, she to collect three buckets of sea water. There is hardly a hint that slavery is ruthless; and their capture lasts little more than a year. Stylistic detachment makes it seem natural that their mother should shout sensible advice to her kidnapped daughter and son across the water, a stunning contrast to the terror experienced by the Tanaka Kinuyo character of the film when they are parted. There is little to suggest that slavery is anything more than loss of liberty and separation from family; Anju and Zushiô long for freedom, but they are never physically abused.

The historical sources are far more brutal. Both children are actually branded and Anju is tortured and killed when her brother escapes. But for Ôgai, the children are only a distressed Hansel and Gretel; not slaves in constant fear of their lives. The fairy-tale elements in his construction are obvious: powerful talismans, separation from parents, parallel but gender-specific experiences, the repetition of the number three, coping with strange surroundings and unfamiliar tasks, the attainment of practical knowledge through the assistance of older strangers. Most of these structural elements do not appear in Ôgai's sources; they are largely his invention and were perhaps influenced by his knowledge of German and Scandinavian folklore.

The mythic unity of the pair is sealed when, unlike the other slaves who are segregated in quarters for men and women, Anju and Zushiô are allowed to remain together in a small shelter of their own. Through this concession, the narrative reinforces the point that the brother and sister are still children. The unity of brother and sister in a world where men and women are separated ensures their innocence and endorses their reluctance to accept maturity. This reluctance reminds us that many fairy-tales are tools to cope with the psychological crisis of growing up. Mizoguchi is uninterested in this crisis; his attention is not on childhood but on the adult struggle for selfhood that follows.

Anju and Zushiô awaken
as adults

The most dramatic divergence between the two works is in the dream-sequence dramatised by Ôgai and completely omitted by Mizoguchi. Their magical sleep secures the children's spiritual alliance but, at the same time, signals the moment of their psychological separation. After one of their captors threatens to punish them with facial branding, both Anju and Zushiô dream that they are branded on the forehead with a hot iron rod. When they pray before Anju's small statue of Jizô, not only is their pain miraculously relieved but their burning wounds completely disappear. When they awaken, they discover that the forehead of the actual Jizô statue now bears two scars. This epiphanous incident ratifies the work's religious purposes, but it also neutralises the savagery of enslavement by confining it to the realm of dreams and imagination.

The society Ôgai envisions need only open its eyes to reform; it wants correction not abolition.[6] The horror of branding escaped slaves is offered as a child's nightmare, not a real experience. Mizoguchi veers sharply from Ôgai in his graphic dramatisation of three incidents that involve the branding and maiming of runaways; his political realism demands that the terrors of the waking world be lived, not merely imagined. It is perhaps telling that the film makes a casual nod to the omitted dream scenario of its source when Zushiô returns as governor to confront Sanshô. His former master says, 'It's like a dream, isn't it? A slave turned governor.'[7]

In the Ôgai version, the grisly dream is for Anju transformative. She is now unusually silent, a signal of the withdrawal at puberty often represented in the fairy-tale as an extended death-like sleep. In her dream-state, Anju leaps past her brother mentally to an intellectual and spiritual realm beyond ordinary language and experience where she can envision escape. Unlike the film, the story emphasises Anju's unusual talent and capability. To carry out the scheme that will free her brother and end her life, she disguises herself as a boy and shaves her head; the change of clothes and loss of hair signal a series of divestitures for Anju that mark the irrevocable loss of her childhood. In Buddhist terms, her male dress is a casting away of the world and its vanities, her shaved head her tonsure in preparation for the salvation it was believed to assure.

The Sanshô story, in all its versions, is always about the power of Anju, but it is a power that can be realised only when it is transferred. Anju's talents and intelligence are efficacious when she gives them up for her brother, who activates them in the political world. Anju relinquishes all that she is and all that she has for the welfare of Zushiô, and more significantly from a Confucian perspective, for the continuity of her family. In 1915, when feminists and intellectuals debated the meaning of the 'new woman', a term that arose after a 1911 production of Ibsen's *A*

Sanshô faces Zushiô as governor (production still)

Doll's House, social conservatives had every reason to remind women of the traditional value of self-sacrifice for brothers, fathers, husbands and sons.

The transfer of her wisdom to her brother is represented by her gift to him of her miraculous statue of Jizô; the amulet eventually ensures Zushiô's re-entry into the public sphere and his worldly success. His appointment as provincial governor reconnects him to his father politically; he wins back the name of his clan Taira and takes his own adult name Masamichi. When his father is pardoned, his posthumous reinstatement realigns Zushiô in the historical continuum. It is important to note that in the Ôgai story Zushiô's success is expressed not as his own achievement but as a natural restoration to his rightful political and familial position. In Confucian thought, class-based male authority is unquestioned; when power is justly ministered, good government is the result, and it has no need for heroes or villains.

The character of Sanshô, as an astonishing example of this norm, is not punished for his crimes, but is rehabilitated and prospers even more, in accordance with neo-Confucian idealisation of correct behaviour and its rewards within a hierarchical system. The rehabilitation of Sanshô is impossible both for the historical sources and in Mizoguchi's film; in all versions other than Ôgai's, Sanshô is vindictively punished. The deletion marks his story as unambiguously Confucian, because its resolution is the triumph of filial piety, the correction of the slaver, and the political reinstatement of the aristocrat.

Why does Ôgai frame a historical tale in a self-consciously objective style but overplay its fairy-tale structure? One reason is because fairy-tales, unlike realistic fiction, are impervious to critique or analysis. The fairy-tale form has mythical authority; it is always convinced of its own correctness and typically ends with an unquestionable sense of resolution. The absence of sentimentality in the narrative works doubly to give its assumptions intellectual legitimacy. Another reason was his wish in his historical fiction to offer not individuals but idealisations, especially idealised women.[8] It is no accident that Ôgai abandoned the present and rewrote a legend of female sacrifice and male *noblesse oblige* at a time when unprecedented class mobility for men and educational opportunities for women undermined Confucian beliefs about the roles of gender and status in the new social structure. At no other time in Japanese history were feminist and democratic ideas so forcefully at work and so fully debated in the press. At just this moment of social crisis, 'Sanshô Dayû' appeared in the literary journal *Chûokôron* and poignantly reminded readers of lost virtues and values that depended on a rigid social hierarchy and conservative views of women. Set in the past, Ôgai's stories were meant as correctives to the liberal excesses of his day. Why else rewrite history, if not to activate it for the present?

Mizoguchi's version of the Sanshô story outstrips ideology by dwelling on the inhumanity of political corruption. His film inverts its source to dwell on individual suffering, rather than on political remedies such as the Imperial rectification of rule that Ôgai proposed. This is not to say that Mizoguchi does not also rewrite history for the political purposes of the present, for his *Sanshô* clearly uses post-war liberalism to correct neo-Confucian ideology. But what sets him apart from Ôgai is that he brings no sense of conviction that his corrective provides a workable alternative to the system his film abolishes. It is the political uncertainty of *Sanshô Dayû* that makes the film an unexpectedly modern melodrama and painfully relevant to 50s Japan.

Sanshô Dayû *as a Melodrama of Post-War Uncertainty*

Not unlike his treatment of Saikaku's *Kôshoku ichidai onna* in *The Life of Oharu* (1952), Mizoguchi manages to uphold his source in *Sanshô Dayû* and to critique it at the same time. There is no doubt of the reverence the film holds for the legend it retells; nonetheless, the Confucian hierarchies of aristocratic rule do not restore the cinematic Zushiô as they do his literary forebear; they defeat him and undermine his idealism. Patrimony does not realign the family to its rightful place of prestige; it expels what remains of them to the desperate shore of history. Sanshô's former slaves do not work harder and prosper under his rehabilitated stewardship; they riot and burn his compound. No temple is erected to Anju's memory; she is commemorated only in the ephemerality of ripples on a pool of water.

Mizoguchi does not simply rework his source, he replenishes the traditionalist 1915 story with the emotionalism, if not the heightened sentimentality, of melodrama, the genre of modernity. He makes no room for epiphanous dreams, magical talismans, disguises, repeated numbers, parallel experiences, helpful strangers or a happy ending. Peter Brooks discusses melodrama in contrast to tragedy as the style's more dignified forebear, but is it not the fairy-tale and its patriarchal views of the family and domesticity that melodrama plays upon and finally rejects? At the heart of every melodrama is an imagined but unattainable happy ending. Melodrama's negation of the fairy-tale arises from its modern refusal to subscribe to the traditional genre's optimism and sense of resolution. In doing away with the sacred myths of a reconstructed past, Mizoguchi invokes in their place a mode of emotional realism that Peter Brooks argues arises in response to the desacralisation of the modern world.[9]

Beyond melodrama but arising from its broken promise of happiness, Mizoguchi's most stunning revision of Ôgai is his invention of the father's liberal idealism – the cause of his exile – summarised in his explanation to his son that all human beings are equal in their right to happiness, an assertion difficult to imagine for a Heian aristocrat. The claim for happiness as a native rather than an imported ideal was on the minds of other film-makers as well in the post-war years. Chishû Ryû, the wise father in Ozu's *Late Spring* (1949), insists to his daughter that the purpose of marriage is to gain individual happiness, an idea inconceivable in Japan before the American Occupation. Masauji's lesson is religious and political. He teaches not only that others deserve happiness but that a ruler must have compassion for others whatever the cost to himself, an ideal that is the director's most radical departure from the traditional Sanshô legend and from the 1915 version. The insertion of ideals inconsonant with medieval ideology generates the modernist tension in the film missing from Ôgai's story.

Significantly, the noble father's idealistic mantra is not merely memorised and repeated; it unlocks the transformative episode in which Zushiô transfers his knowledge to Tarô, the good son of the wicked bailiff. In a brilliant stroke of dramatisation, Mizoguchi makes strategic use of a face-to-face meeting between sons of characters who represent moral polarities – one epitomises evil, the other benevolence.[10] Zushiô instructs Tarô according to his own father's ethics: 'It is compassion that makes us human. Even if you yourself suffer, you must have compassion for others.' Tarô's subsequent flight from the slave-compound to a monastery exquisitely symbolises the desire for an impossible transcendence that Brooks identifies as a condition for melodrama. But in the sons' encounter, Mizoguchi positions himself squarely among the 'melodramatists [who] refuse to allow that the world has been completely drained of transcendence; and [who] locate that transcendence in the struggle of the children of light with the children of darkness, in the play of the ethical mind'.[11] Each son will defy or fail his father; and each operates in a world made more immanent by failure and defiance, while their fathers occupy a realm of mythic tragedy.

The members of the aristocratic family are each separately dramatised as teachers; here Zushiô passes along the lessons of his father and mother, but even Anju will gently tutor a new slave in the humble lessons of both weaving and kindness. With these episodes the film schools us in the transformative effects of the lone moral exemplar, even if the teachers themselves derive few tangible benefits from their knowledge. It is a mark of Mizoguchi's story-telling mastery that he trumps his source text by adding to it the stipulation that Zushiô pass along his father's words to someone else, that is, that he activate his father's impossible ideal in the everyday discourse of human exchange. Had he not, the precept would remain the privileged possession of an insightful nobleman rather than the film's transactive moral force. In Ôgai's story, Tarô's repulsion is enough to make him walk away from evil; but Mizoguchi constructs a world that operates on motivations more profound than disgust. Once he is in possession of the ideal of compassion he can no longer remain in the society of slaves, a microcosm of the profane world of commodification. The words of Zushiô's father give the slave-holder's son an ethical framework for the natural repugnance he experiences at his own father's brutality.

But something even more dire is at stake in this exchange. Soon after he teaches Sanshô's son his father's memorised precept, Zushiô will descend into a darkness that banishes the practical validity of his exiled father's doctrine. Moral obscurity is thematic from the outset, announced in the opening inter-title, a warning that the story comes from an unenlightened era when men 'had not yet opened their eyes to other men as human beings'. Accordingly, darkness interrupts the film at significant intervals to envelop Anju and Zushiô in reminders of the external forces against which they strive. Dark transitions metaphorically imply Mizoguchi's rejection of Ôgai's optimistic interpretation of the Sanshô story, most notably in fades to black that punctuate the first half of the film. One significantly occurs after the children are abandoned in their sleep by Tarô.

The intensity of the film's emotional darkness encourages a reading of the dimmed screen as a compressed allegory for both their stolen childhood and the eradication of ethical rule. The fade to black here works doubly as narrative shift and moral metaphor. But more than transition or symbol, this standard cinematic device effectively elides the childhood and redemptive dream-sequences pivotal to Ôgai's version and so becomes a prominent metaphor for Mizoguchi's post-war revision of the text that fathers his own. Taken together with the film's liberalism, the elision blots out the 'dream' of neo-Confucian militarism, through which a generation of Japanese in the 30s and 40s, Mizoguchi's viewers, had fitfully 'slept'.

Before Tarô leaves, he covers the slumbering children, 'concealing' the Ôgai version that contains the romanticised story of the childhood that Mizoguchi subsumes. When the screen lightens, the round foundation stones that marked the beginning of the film are again referenced, a mysterious image signalling the regrounding of the narrative in the past, followed by Zushiô and Anju's awakening as adults.[12] This interval, which amounts to a ten-year night, is a perverse inversion of the enchanted sleep of fairy-tales, and of the epiphanous dream-sleep that marks the children's enlightenment central to Ôgai's story. In fairy-tales, the suspension of time that magical sleep allows fulfils the adolescent fantasy of maturity postponed, but no such deferment is possible in the film. Anju and Zushiô open their eyes not to claim the benevolent realm their father envisioned but to resume the routine savagery of their capture.

The film takes pains to present them as 'adult children', grown but as inviolate as when Tarô left them, for brother and sister still sleep apart from the other slaves and together in the same hut, their bodies modestly arranged head to head. The implication of presenting them as we left them is that, although the children have grown older, they have waited psychologically for the film to catch up with them. Once they awaken, the differentiation of their personalities proceeds rapidly. The 'very next morning', as it were, Zushiô proves that he learned his father's words only by rote and not by heart when he brands the forehead of a recaptured slave. He carries out the same act of cruelty that Tarô, his childhood pupil, refused to do, within the implied time-frame of the film, only 'the night before'. Anju's horror demonstrates that nothing has prepared her for her brother's savagery, a signal that the sleep interval, where Ôgai's rich version of their childhood resides, is empty of narrative content. Time has passed but nothing has happened.

Zushiô becomes Sanshô's 'son' when he brands a fellow slave

His act also subtly implies an impending threat to Anju's inviolability. If Anju's brother has the capacity to mutilate another human being, how can she expect the protection her isolation with him has guaranteed up to now? The vulnerability always under the surface of Mizoguchi's film is entirely missing from Ôgai's story. His version avoids the obvious conclusion that the kidnappers have sold the children's mother into prostitution. She does not reappear in the narrative until her reunion with Zushiô and there is no mention of what happened to her during that interval. Mizoguchi's realism will not tolerate this cleansing omission and goes further to insist that Tamaki's fate unavoidably prefigures her daughter's destiny as a slave. Zushiô acknowledges her vulnerability when he reminds her that she will surely end up in a brothel

Tamaki crippled by her captors

should they escape. Once her brother has fled she will be tortured and perhaps killed; but the more important implication of his escape is that without Zushiô she will become the sexual prey of her overseers. Anju's purity gives meaning to the urgency and dignity of her suicide.

The branding episode reinterprets the earlier scene of Tarô's departure; at that moment, exquisitely undramatised and underplayed, the son of the bailiff and the son of the aristocrat trade places. They exchange their lives, their legacies, and most significantly, their father's values one for the other. The substitution is sealed when Tarô renames Zushiô 'Mutsu', for the barbarian place of his birth. The renaming reminds us of the fragility of our own identities and how hard it is to win our true names, or as Stanley Cavell puts it, to find our way to 'the name of the kind to which one is kin'.[13] Zushiô's shifting appellations (he becomes a slave named Mutsu and then a governor restored to his patriarchal title Taira no Masamichi) predict that he will never fully reclaim the name that by the end of the film is known only to his blind mother.

The disfigurement that appears so prominently in all versions of the Sanshô story is a perverse inversion of the power of naming, identity and knowability. Disfigurement takes the place of the internalisation of individuality achieved in claiming the name to which one is kin. Slave-master Sanshô replaces identity with an isolating mark, the sign of the outcast that prevents re-entry in society. The power of naming and its distortion also reveal why this story has the 'wrong' name, that is, why it is known as 'Sanshô Dayû', and not 'Anju and Zushiô'. The story actually has exactly the right title, within the perverse logic of identity that the narrative enacts, for Sanshô is the only character who does not lose or change his name. He is the only character free to name himself. Epitomising 'the Tyrant of some Asiatick Isle the only free man in an Island of Slaves',[14] he achieves his name and his freedom by his extermination of the integrity and individuality of others.

His mother's blindness in the final scene is part of fate's conspiracy against Zushiô's retrieval of his lost identity. It is the melodramatic ache at the heart of this story that Zushiô's mother will never see him, despite their reunion, but it is a deeper existential torment that he experiences by her initial inability, and her symbolic refusal, to recognise him. This unexpected turn (there has been no premonition earlier in the film that Tamaki will lose her sight) reinforces an interpretation of her blindness

Tamaki's blindness
conspires against her
recognition of Zushiô

as a psychological 'misrecognition' of her son, who needs her – the only survivor who knows his true name – to confirm who he is. It is his mother's misrecognition, an excessive injury even within this film, that turns not just this scene but the entire work into melodrama, the mode of excess.[15]

We are forced to imagine the humiliating taunts that provoke his mother first to tell him, 'You won't fool me again,' but we are moreover forced to realise what Zushiô faces: he not only goes unseen by his mother, he remains unknown to himself forever. At this moment occurs the final separation between Anju and Zushiô. By asking for her daughter, Tamaki convinces us that, had she survived, Anju could not have gone unrecognised. Her capacity to be recognised, to achieve the identity 'of the kind to which she is kin' resides in her inviolable integrity. Anju, renamed Shinobu for her endurance and faithful memory, never loses herself, never forgets who she is. In contrast, Zushiô becomes an eternal stranger, nameless and lost to himself and the world forever. This loss is the exaggeration of melodrama, an excess signalled by the rise of the camera away from the figures on the cliff and to an indifferent sweep across the shore.

That sweep returns us emotionally to the point earlier in the film when Tamaki hobbles to this same cliff on Sado Island to call her children once more. Visually, this is the most intense scene in the film; Tamaki's hair whipped by the wind across her face is an eloquent recapitulation of her suffering. This interlude is also the film's most aurally copious scene, an excessiveness that heightens the melodramatic discordances of the film.

Four distinct sound threads surround her. As her friends carry her toward the bluff where she can look across the sea to Echigo, the ambient sound of the waves mingles with the twang of a samisen, the traditional instrument of the courtesan entertainer. The samisen is distinctly ironic here. Its music is associated with the entertainment women provide for men; as a context for Tamaki the atonal notes are a taunting reminder of her sexual enslavement. Over these two sound-lines rises the orchestral 'Zushiô–Anju' melody of the mother's song, a refrain we never actually hear Tamaki sing, but which is intoned for Anju by a sister-slave from Sado. The emotionalism of the strains of the maternal song interweaves with the seductive music of the brothel. As Tamaki reaches the top of the bluff alone, the swell of the ocean gives way to baleful winds. Above these sounds, Tamaki calls out, 'Zushiô-oo! Anju-uu! Anju-uu! Zushiô-oo!' her tremulous voice trailing out to sea. The interweaving of these four separate patterns of sound – vocal, natural, orchestral and atonal – comprises the operatic 'melos', or emotional song of melodrama.

These intermingled sentiments depend on the scene just prior, in which Anju begins the melodic progression by weaving the slave-girl's song to the sound of her mother's voice. The legendary Anju is more resourceful than Mizoguchi allows, though he retains in her characterisation her moral superiority to secure her place in mythic tradition. The sibling pair, with strong sister and wayward brother, has its origin in the Japanese creation myth of Izanagi and Izanami, but is more immediately referenced in the solar deity Amaterasu and her mischievous brother Susano-o. Rooted in Japanese mythology is the concept of the capable and civilising sister who must tame or outwit her wild brother to achieve peace and social stability. This fundamentality of the brother–sister pairing is played out in the kinds of labour Mizoguchi has Anju and Zushiô perform. Like Amaterasu, Anju spins thread and weaves cloth, traditional female activities that bring materials together, to consolidate and unify. Zushiô, on the other hand, works as a blacksmith; he subjects metals to fire, hammer and tong. He reshapes what he touches by brute force and in the process transforms himself into a brute. Like Susano-o he is a destroyer who will be reformed by his sister's civilising influence.

But Anju is more than a maker of cloth, she is a weaver of souls. It is consonant with the design of the film that she is teaching the techniques of spinning and weaving when she hears her pupil and sister-slave sing her own mother's song. Anju is the one who interlaces the lost strands of her family by tying her mother in her heart to her own intoned name. Zushiô refuses to accept this 'news from home' as Anju untangles the riddle that reweaves them to their mother. Zushiô's doubt at this moment marks the depth of his estrangement from the self that his sister tries to resummon. Anju alone, by her unfailing memory and integrity, can authorise the song that names the 'names to which they are kin'. As already noted, naming and calling are essential to the primary purpose of the film. The fact that Anju and Zushiô are invited to hearken to the call of their names to win their lost identities is a reminder that responsiveness is a constitutive feature in the attainment of the mature self — a self in dialogue with others.

Naming and response are tenets of Jôdo or Pure Land Buddhism, the most important emerging sect at the time of the original legend, the largest sect in Japan today, and the doctrinal system that provides the film's philosophical basis. The sect teaches that the invocation of the name of Amida contains both his call and the believer's response to true life. Mizoguchi translates that religious practice into a secular metaphor for an identity retrieved in the call to oneself in the voice of another.

Expressive of Jôdo belief, the Sanshô story stipulates that the achievement of salvation requires the aid of another. Jôdo Buddhism relies on the intervention of Amida, resident Buddha of the Pure Land;

and unlike Zen's belief in self-reliance, the sect teaches the near impossibility of achieving release from the cycle of death and rebirth on one's own. Amida is attended by the Bodhisattva Kannon, 'the one who hears their cries', who is the personification of infinite compassion depicted in the amulet Zushiô carries. *Sanshô Dayû* is about intercession, intervention and self-sacrifice, enacted in the film's requirement that every liberation comes through the help of another. Tarô's conversion and release

Anju resummons Zushiô's faith (production still)

demand the surrender of Zushiô's identity and moral potential; in turn, Zushiô's freedom demands the death of Anju.

Anju's excitement at the words of her mother's song expresses the joy of recognition, of hearing and responding to the call of one's true self, a metaphysical recognition. Anju's weaving together of threads of information about their mother and her attempt to engage Zushiô in the significance of that information acknowledge the act of responsiveness as a condition for the integrity of the self. This integrity rests on basic beliefs in family and its foundational position for humane community, a condition absent or perpetually under threat in a company of slaves. *Sanshô Dayû* takes as its subject the scattering of a family because it is the family in society that first responds to the basic human desire for connectedness with others and identification with them.[16] The drama of the story is not the break-up of the family itself but how the two children separately deal with that crisis as a struggle for identity-with-others in an underworld that mocks their desire for genuine connection.

Anju binds her family together but, more profoundly, her responsiveness entwines the human and the spiritual. In an artless act of compassion, she places in the hands of a dying bondswoman, who is about to be abandoned in a bone-yard, a rope that she ties to a worn Buddhist image carved in stone. This physical connection with the icon expresses the simplicity of the faith of the downtrodden for whom Jôdo Buddhism had

the greatest appeal. The sect promises the potential universality of salvation, a potential unavailable in the reliance of the so-called esoteric sects on arcane ritual and in Zen on meditation and enlightenment. Anju, like Kannon, the avatar of compassion her father reveres, reconnects those in despair to the promise of faith. In folk expressions of Buddhist belief, images aid the adherent to conceptualise the Pure Land and the redemptive power of the intervening Bodhisattva.

Anju joins Namiji to Buddha with a rope (production still)

Sanshô Dayû itself can be understood as a religious artwork, a film that participates in the rich Japanese tradition of Buddhist sculpture and illustration. The film takes its place as a meditative icon, a heuristic for the depiction of doctrine akin to the highly detailed paintings and realistic statuary of the period in which the film is set. Mizoguchi sculpts in celluloid images of faith as powerful as ancient depictions of exemplary monks and nuns, whose portraits of spirituality authorise the film's medieval assertion that a religious life is a genuine antidote to a corrupt world.

Jizô and Kannon are the most beloved Bodhisattvas in Japanese Buddhist tradition and it is instructive that Ôgai chooses one and Mizoguchi the other. The director deliberately and effectively exchanges Ôgai's Jizô, protector of children, for Kannon, Bodhisattva of compassion, to reinforce the location of the story in the realm of adults. In the film, the amulet is not Anju's magical possession, but it is Zushiô's sign of his father's word, rule and legacy. No doubt Mizoguchi rejected the sword Zushiô carries in Ôgai's story as an impossible symbol for benevolent governance in post-war Japan. But reminiscences of the sword remain. We never see the younger Zushiô when he is not brandishing something: in the childhood scenes a toy straw horse, in adolescence a knife, and in adulthood an iron rod and a scythe. In contrast, the amulet hangs from his neck untouched until it is discarded, more albatross than empowering talisman, a problematic inheritance to be escaped rather than cherished as a key to liberation. When Zushiô rips the amulet from his neck and throws it to the ground after Anju reveals the potential for contact with their mother, he is freed of his father's legacy, but is finally fully enslaved.

From where does Anju derive her unassailable faith and wisdom when her brother betrays their noble birthright? The transference is subtle but is no less profound than her father's formal instruction to Zushiô on the night before his exile. As he departs the next day, one of the last things he says is to the infant Anju. 'Grow up quickly,'[17] he tells her, expressing the parental wish, typical of the time, that his daughter reach adulthood before the vagaries of childhood can harm her. We also understand these words, his only words to Anju, as a prescient warning that she will be called upon to grow up too quickly when she is kidnapped and sold. Her father's gentle plea legitimises her position as guardian of the family legacy her brother will betray.

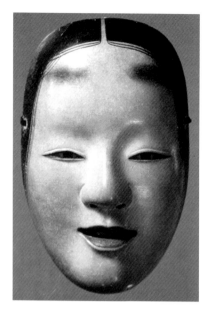

A more poetic and dire transfer comes to Anju from her mother. At the end of the first flashback, when the father's exile is explained, the camera moves slightly behind and above the head of Tamaki. The curve of her pale cheek and its echo in the classic contour of her coiffure immediately connote the Heian heroine, the female repository of elegance, aristocratic grace and aesthetic knowledge. Hers is the classic late-Heian face, a stoic Noh mask filled with restrained emotion, reminiscent of the mother in the play *Sumidagawa*, who travels in search of a child she will learn has died. A fade to the present finds Tamaki far from her noble home and poised at the edge of a forest stream, an image that in context conjures another classical intertext. 'The flow of the river is ceaseless but the water is never the same,' wrote Kamo no Chômei at the opening of the *Hôjôki*, a late-Heian essay and early expression of Jôdo belief, extolling the Buddhist call to relinquish one's possessions in the face of political instability and the uncertainties of life on earth. Dispossessed of home and husband Tamaki exemplifies the suffering the *Hôjôki* describes.

Tamaki fills a bowl of water from the stream, water that suggests the clarity of her memory. She is unaware that it is only in retrospection that her husband will survive. Significantly, it is for Anju that she has drawn the water and, as she passes it to her daughter, she transfers to her both past and future. Tamaki bequeaths the memory of her husband to the child and at

Top Classic Heian beauty and serenity captured in a Noh mask
Below A travelling mother separated from her child in the Noh play *Sumidagawa*

the same time foretells her daughter's watery suicide. The circle of water prefigures the round ripples that will mark her sacrificial death for Zushiô, whose recollection of their father's precept has initiated the flashback. When Anju drinks the water, metaphorically accepting her fate, she closes the circle her brother opened when he asked their mother questions about their father's lost status and banishment.

Anju is the fixed centre of meaning, authorised in the undisturbed circles that expand across the surface of the water at the point of her drowning. A succession of interrogatories has led to this unspoken answer: a boy asks the details of his father's history, peasants ask the reason for their lord's exile, a mother asks the reason for a law that denies her children shelter, a slaver's son asks about compassion, Anju asks the words of a song, and Zushiô asks in despair the reason for faith in a faithless world. The

Top The clarity of memory reflected in a bowl of water
Below Tamaki transfers both past and future to Anju

Anju's sacrificial suicide

A witness at the gateway
between slavery and
salvation

Anju's death marks the
fixed centre of meaning

answer is more than the various replies they receive; it is the response that Anju's courage makes to the voice that calls her to become who she is.[18] Like Kannon, Anju is 'the one who hears their cries', in her literal ability to hear the meaning of the slave-girl's song, to hear the suffering pleas of her fellow slaves, and to 'hear' and comprehend the meaning of her mother's voice. In the bone-yard where the living meet the dead, Anju hears the call but Zushiô does not, for it is not their mother's voice at all, but her own, the voice of an internal 'mother' that is the origination of her own transformation. Zushiô cannot hear the call because he cannot hear the mothering voice that calls within him to become 'who he is'.

Anju's search for Tamaki ends when she becomes the mother of her own and Zushiô's liberation. She convinces him to escape without her in a plan that defies logic, first saying that only one of them has a chance of avoiding recapture, and then instructing him to carry the dying Namiji to safety, a far greater encumbrance to his flight. Zushiô's stubbornness can no longer resist Anju's faith. His hard-won pragmatism is his defence no longer, for it has given way to a harder-won compassion. Anju actualises their father's command for compassion when she offers to sacrifice herself not only for her brother but for the humblest of human beings, an old and dying sister-slave. When Zushiô hoists Namiji on his back he takes up the burden of compassion that Anju has prepared for him and demonstrates that his father's ideal is not merely a sentiment one feels, but an obligation one must enact against cynicism and self-gain. Zushiô is already designated by the film as an actor and activator – recall the instruments he flourishes in every scene to cut and forge – and so he is fated not to experience meaning within, as Anju does, but to act out and activate the significance of his family's sacrifice in the political world.

At Anju's death, the film recaptures the lost meaning of her father's courage to be 'who he is' and only marks time from that moment forward to allow the narrative to fill itself in through Zushiô's series of retrievals. He saves Namiji, becomes governor, pays homage to his dead father, returns to rescue his sister, learns of her death, begs forgiveness from the slave he branded, emancipates the Sanshô slaves, and at last discovers his mother in the place of their final abandonment. The film ends as it began, with son and mother far from home and dispossessed. Anju, unknowable but eternally free, is at the fixed and meaningful centre of the endless circle Zushiô's journey traces back to his beginning, a metaphor for the Buddhist doctrine of the painful cycle of life, death and rebirth. We should remind ourselves that Buddhist rebirth is not redemptive, unless it is in the Pure Land promised by Jôdo belief: reincarnation in the human realm is an inescapable vale of tears. Weeping, Zushiô buries his head in his mother's womb, acknowledging his return to it, acquiescing to the karmic cycle that enslaves him. Anju remains at the still centre opposing the line of story and of mundane history, opposing the movement that is narrative film itself, opposing us, inscribed as awed and distant watchers in the witness of her friend who prays for her. When Anju breathes her last, all the oxygen goes out of the film. In Anju's suicide *Sanshô Dayû* reaches too deftly and in spite of itself a site of meaning so irreducible that the film has nothing left to say.

Conclusion for an Endless Legend

It is the centrality and unknowability of Anju that make Stanley Cavell's *Contesting Tears: The Hollywood Melodrama of the Unknown Woman* resonate with *Sanshô Dayû*. The generic features in the 'melodramas of unknownness' that Cavell specifies are prominent in Mizoguchi's film despite its own defiance of anything as simple as genre. In the unknown woman films the father is absent, the mother or a search for the mother is always present, 'the past is frozen, mysterious, with topics forbidden and isolating', and the action ends where it began, that is, in a place not of perspective but of 'abandonment or transcendence'.[19] Melodramas of unknownness meditate on women who sacrifice themselves for their families, or for desired families.[20] Similarities of absence, mystery, abandonment, transcendence and connection point to a kinship, if not a generic connection, between *Sanshô* and this group of American films.[21] What makes these resemblances worth mentioning is not that they mistakenly allow us to force Mizoguchi's film into an American genre, or to make some misguided claim for influence, but that they unexpectedly reveal something fundamental about Japanese film, similar to a claim Cavell makes for American movies.

He argues that motion pictures have played in the United States a role different from their role in other cultures, and this difference is a function of the absence in the United States of the European edifice of philosophy. American film participates in the 'Western cultural ambition of self-thought and self-invention that presents itself in that absence'.[22] Movies are pressured by American culture to satisfy the craving for thought, 'the ambition of a talented culture to examine itself publicly'.[23]

The same assertion is surprisingly valid for Japanese film. No edifice of philosophy is prominent in Japan, as in Europe and China, and so it has been the task, historically, of literature to satisfy the Japanese 'craving for thought', for self-contemplation and public examination. The I-novels that Mori Ôgai wrote against in writing 'Sanshô Dayû' argue convincingly that the cultural ambition of self-thought and self-invention is not exclusively Western; and the eleventh-century *Tale of Genji* goes a long way to argue that this native ambition pre-dates twentieth-century modernity. 'The role of literature and the visual arts in Japanese culture is of enormous importance,' writes Katô Shûichi, because 'in every age of their history, the Japanese have expressed their thought not so much in abstract philosophical systems as in concrete literary works.'[24] Film takes up the tasks of painting and writing to fulfil the ambitions of an absent philosophy, in conditions unexpectedly similar to those in the United States and under the pressures of a similarly talented culture in demand of a location for self-thought.

In both American and Japanese cinema there is an over-reliance on genre, because, following Cavell's claim, the membership relations that films in a genre produce mask their individual strivings toward self-contemplation. There is another telling point of resemblance: the philosophical import of both national film groups has gone unrecognised by native audiences (who, in the American case, Cavell claims, 'lack the means to grasp this thought as such for the very reason that [they] naturally or historically lack the edifice of philosophy within which to grasp it')[25] and both have relied on European critics for that initial recognition (Mizoguchi 'discovered' by the French is an example). The similar philosophical conditions of American and Japanese film account for the uncanny familiarity some critics in the United States sensed when they saw Japanese films for the first time in the 50s and 60s, despite profound cultural differences.

It would be a mistake to assume that Mizoguchi's film is defined by genre. The resemblances are illuminating for what they reveal about the import of *Sanshô Dayû* and its registration of the melodramatic, but the film nonetheless does not follow faithfully the features of Cavell's melodrama of the unknown woman. For example, there is no repudiation of the father possible for Anju, though the father is no less problematic here than in the unknown woman films. Questions about the nature of those problems return us to Mizoguchi's project, the repudiation of his own 'father', as it were, Mori Ôgai. Mizoguchi directs his film against an ancestral Ôgai, not out of anxiety, but with unprecedented confidence that history must be overthrown to repudiate the ideology that fathered the Pacific War.

The film stakes its position in its anti-Confucian reinterpretation of the father, Masauji. The original Heian legend, the early twentieth-century short-story and the mid-century film differ significantly in the reason for the father's exile. In the original, he is banished because of an unnamed offence against a temple. The Ôgai version implicates him in a crime committed by the governor of the province where he serves and implies that he accepts his punishment in loyalty to his superior. It should be noted that the extension of the punishment from the governor to his ministers is in itself a Confucian concept. In the film, the father is clearly innocent of any crime, though there can be no doubt that he is guilty of undermining traditional ideology, a transgression that fundamentally isolates him from his peers. He is punished not only because his ideals are at odds with military misrule, but more significantly, because they go against social hierarchy. Mizoguchi invents a modern political character in Masauji, an individualised and liberal man who is punished for values that transcend social norms. Such characters do not exist in the Japanese tradition.

But the crisis of exile figures prominently in that tradition. Numerous and extended references to banishment in Heian (794–1185) literary works indicate that it was a punishment used not only to penalise wrongdoing but to eliminate political opponents on trumped-up charges. The death sentence was not imposed after the early ninth century when exile became by default the severest punishment under Japanese law. In the eleventh and twelfth centuries banishment often came with the confiscation of the exile's land. Whole genres of poetry and prose grew up around the plight of the noble exile, whose banishment and its trials stamp him as a hero. By the eleventh century, exile becomes an expected part of the literary construction of the noble hero, as is clear when the Shining Genji imposes the punishment on himself for a secret crime.[26] The Sanshô legend is different from the paradigm in that the story dwells not on the noble exile himself but on those he has been forced to leave behind. The story concerns itself with the consequences of wrongdoing or political misfortune rather than on the opportunities for romance or heroism banishment affords. The legend is an archaic morality tale, told to warn those who govern of the misfortune imprudent action may bring not only upon themselves but on those they hold most dear, rather than the sophisticated romance of exile that later emerged.

It is not difficult to argue that all of the unhappiness of Mizoguchi's version of *Sanshô Dayû* is traceable to the mistakes of parents. Sanshô himself is an obvious caricature of the evil paterfamilias, who distorts the virtue of filial piety by demanding his son commit a heinous act of cruelty to demonstrate his loyalty. Masauji represents a father more complex and more resistant to interpretation, but one who must bear the blame of his family's destruction. He is not simply 'un modèle du Bien';[27] he is, on the contrary, the site of two opposing value systems that each offer an ethical alternative, and which cannot exist side by side. This opposition makes Masauji entirely modern, and it is with this difficult modernity that Zushiô actually struggles.

As wise father and benign ruler, Masauji exemplifies enlightened Confucian authority; his only concern is for the well-being of those in his care. He follows the principle of Kongjuzi (Confucius) who told the wicked Governor of Lu, 'If you desire what is good, the people will at once be good' (*Analects* 12:19). Masauji is validated in his desire for good by the uncompromising affection the peasants have for him. Masauji's individualised idealism is at war with this principle; his desire for good expresses itself idiosyncratically because it actually opposes Confucian hierarchy, in its modern desire for individual happiness and equality. Recall the rabble of peasants who invade his garden in tandem with the threatening soldiers who occupy his sitting-room. These simultaneous incursions represent the conflict between his private ideals and public expectations, and it is no accident that the confrontation takes place in his home and in the presence of his family, for they are the ones he has put into jeopardy.

Masauji has blurred the boundaries between public and private by allowing his personal hopes to spill into his public administration, with the result that he has left his family vulnerable. It is a cardinal rule of Japanese ethics that one must suppress one's own desires for the welfare of those to whom one is obligated, and Masauji has a far more sacred duty to his family than to the farmers he governs. Even his desire for transcendent good is a personal desire nonetheless, and as his uncle angrily reminds him, should not have been allowed to interfere with fatherly responsibility. Zushiô will receive a similarly stern warning about the error of his personal values from the benevolent prime minister. Masuji's philosophy is essentially personal and so is misguided in Confucian thinking for its promotion of individual happiness. The film refuses to sentimentalise his idealism; his values ruin his family and in the end do nothing to help the peasants. Caught between two ethical systems, Masauji is destroyed.

The problematic riot scene after the liberation of the Sanshô slaves goes even further to mock the ideal that Zushiô tries to enact, for it mirrors the chaotic scene of rebellious peasants storming his father's home. The difference between Ôgai and Mizoguchi is most striking in the mêlée, an incident that does not, and indeed could not, occur in the short-story. In contrast to Mizoguchi, Ôgai endorses neo-Confucian orthodoxy by assuring the reader that, once they have been liberated, the former slaves work harder than ever for the rehabilitated Sanshô. No riot or retribution, only correct rule. The film, in contrast, chooses realism over orthodoxy by imagining what real slaves would do once their enslaver has been overthrown. The film makes the strong point that Sanshô and the military are one, and so we are encouraged to imagine that when the emancipated slaves riot against his rule, they rebel against the enslaving militarism of the twentieth century. It is not difficult to imagine Mizoguchi, once a young

Masauji caught between private ideals and public obligations

leftist and always on the side of the oppressed, among them. He revolts against his 'ancestor' Ôgai, against the shackles of history, and against the fathering ideology of Japanese militarism. Mizoguchi does not rebel against the traditions of civilisation, but against the fascist politicians and generals who usurped it for their own uncivilised ends. Here Mizoguchi and Zushiô merge as revolutionaries in the cause of a modernity that will in the end fail them, a modernity that, like Masauji, tries impossibly to reconcile two opposing systems. It is the cause of men exiled from history and doomed to wander between an inoperable ideology and an impossible ideal. Zushiô's foreclosed allegiance to two values in conflict makes him Mizoguchi's most modern hero.

As much as Mizoguchi may have intended his *Sanshô Dayû* to be the final and definitive version of the tale, it will no doubt be recounted in novel modes and different versions as history demands. If the course of the Sanshô legend runs true, Mizoguchi's film predicts its own overthrow. A new interpretation of the devotions that bind the scattered family of the Sanshô narrative will no doubt displace Mizoguchi's ancestral film. A new revolutionary will emerge to retell the tale for a new time and a new ideal. Twice-told in the twentieth century at critical moments of political

Freed slaves celebrate the end of militarist misrule

39

change, the legend will be as ready in other centuries to provide a private ground for public struggle. But in all its future modes, one thing is certain. The story will always imagine the passionate faith and affections of a mother, a father, a sister and a brother in an enduring relationship to one another, unbroken by the ideologies their plight is used to represent.

The endurance of the family enshrined by Mizoguchi in waves of grass

MIZO DAYÛ

....

Dudley Andrew

'Mizoguchi the Master' was the title of the centennial retrospective organised in 1998 by the Japan Foundation.[28] 'Master' signifies someone at the summit of an art or craft; it also carries the less agreeable connotation of paternalism, as in 'slave-master'. 'Mizo Dayû' is equally ambivalent. Mizoguchi is the 'Bailiff', serving tradition as its implacable cinematic overseer. But 'Dayû' also means 'professional story-teller', one through whom legends are revivified.[29] This is the role Carole Cavanaugh highlighted, seeing the legend of 'Sanshô', with its scarcely locatable origin, pass through Mizoguchi's telling on its way to an indefinite future. Such is the nature of any fertile legend, I too begin by saying. But I end quite differently, on the closing down of the legend in the finale of Mizoguchi's version, a version which, though perhaps not definitive, appears – in all senses of the term – conclusive.

Where the longevity and deployment of the 'Sanshô' tale inside Japan are unmistakable, so too has been that tale's increasing internationalisation via Mizoguchi retrospectives around the globe. In 1994

Criterion issued a variorum laser disc of *Sanshô Dayû*, making use of the scholarly research on the legend commissioned by the American film-maker Terrence Malick. Few were aware of Malick's short-lived adaptation of the film for the New York stage in 1994 until a still from the Mizoguchi movie appeared in the Sunday *New York Times* feature on *The Thin Red Line*.[30] Now it is rumoured that Malick may remake *Sanshô Dayû*.

This dynamic afterlife substantiates the two related themes that run through Mizoguchi's version: the theme of ritual narration which makes possible the theme of survival. As for the film's survival, the critics at *Cahiers du Cinéma* had much to do with that. They ranked *Sanshô Dayû* as the top film of 1960, the year of its Paris release, ahead of *L'avventura*, *A bout de souffle* (*Breathless*) and *Tirez sur le pianiste* (*Shoot the Piano Player*) in that order. They applauded the purity of its construction, the mature wisdom of its narration. And yet they sensed something fresh about Mizoguchi's story-telling, a 'tableau primitif',[31] wherein you could sense the rebirth of cinema. A tale of origins, *Sanshô Dayû* is set at so remote a time that Mizoguchi could imagine himself returning to the rudiments of both morality and narrative art at one and the same stroke. The urge to renew himself and his art through 'Sanshô' welled up in Terrence Malick as it did in Mizoguchi, a paradoxical urge given the familiarity of the story. This chapter likewise aims to return to a basic conception of the cinema by refreshing what is familiar in Mizoguchi's masterful film, following his own route to the origin of what is valuable only in repetition.

Mysterious traces
harbouring ancient legends

The Legend and the Legendary
Recall the opening shot: the ruined stumps of columns of an ancient manor, over them appears a scripted title whose literal translation should read:

> The origin of this legend of 'Sanshô the Bailiff' goes back to the Heian period when mankind had not yet opened their eyes to other men as human beings. It has been retold by the people for centuries and is treasured today as one of the epic folk tales of our history.[32]

In determining to return to these dark ages and to perpetuate this legend Mizoguchi surely had his own moment in mind, the humiliating decade 1944–54. An account of that decade by Shunsuke Tsurumi contains a telling anecdote:

> During the last stage of the war, a novelist recruited for compulsory labor service commented that his way of carrying earth in a crude straw basket seemed like a return to the age of the gods as told in the legend. Our manner of living at the outset of the occupation had much in common with the ancients.[33]

The legend referred to might as well be Mizoguchi's *Sanshô Dayû*, where characters do haul wood on their backs and where we are told the foundations of civilisation are not yet in place.

Yet the nobility of *Sanshô Dayû*'s images and music exudes a certain longing for this cruel, chaotic era, perhaps because it was foundational. We know that as soon after the war as the American censors permitted – indeed even before they permitted – Mizoguchi immersed himself and his audiences in earlier periods, skirting their interdictions against period films in his biography of the eighteenth-century artist Utamaro (1946). With the occupiers gone but with modernity rising from the rubble like a soaring skyscraper, this time he travelled further back in history than he had ever gone. Tsurumi claims that at the onset of the Occupation in 1945, Japanese art was at the 'cave painting' stage. Mizoguchi must have felt closer to the bold designs of such elemental expression than to the everyday realism that was beginning to pour from television sets, introduced commercially in Japan in 1954. He recounts *Sanshô Dayû* in an ancient manner. His characters (the tyrant, the dutiful daughter, the greedy official, the kidnappers) derive from a folkloric style that dispenses with the fussy psychologism of modern fiction. Mizoguchi delivers a bold 'cave painting' suitable to the primitive situation to which the war and Occupation had reduced this culture. His film aims to be as fundamental as a legend.

Legends store primitive power that can be called up as required but that no adaptation exhausts. Gilles Deleuze writes of beleaguered peoples inventing themselves by 'making up legends'. If one takes Japan as a nation that during the Occupation became invisible to itself – when the United States prevented the past from being seen and revoked customs and traditions – then *Sanshô Dayû* could be said to call this people to consciousness. After three years of a Korean conflict in which Japan was used as a staging area, many Japanese must have felt inducted into an international drama scripted by the United States. Legends rally suppressed, 'pre-existent peoples'. Deleuze writes: 'To catch people in the act of making up legends is to apprehend the movement of a people's constitution.'[34] Was Mizoguchi among the anti-modernists who considered themselves an insurgent *minority* of this sort and who wanted to recover the *majority* discourse of a healthy nationalism that had been hijacked by the military in 1931 and then suppressed by the Americans in 1945? *Sanshô Dayû* represents Japan as created by a 'pre-existent people' and challenges modern Japanese to resemble their ancient ancestors.

In this Mizoguchi can be said to follow the lead of the celebrated anthropologist Yanagita Kunio who, early in the century, recorded tales of the mountainous regions where he believed uncorrupted Japanese origins lay dormant. Questioning modernisation, prescribing a prophylaxis against its encroachments, Yanagita mined the lore of the Tôno district in northeastern Honshû, publishing a famous anthology of legends in 1910. Five years later, he took up the Sanshô tale, just after Mori Ôgai had brought out his sensationally popular version.[35] To Yanagita, 'Sanshô' is the kind of tale that springs from mountain sources (it opens in his beloved Tôno area) and should flow down to the corrupted central cities. Not that he fought modern technology. Indeed Yanagita took heart in the rail system that had united the country and that could bring rural values in from the periphery to Tokyo Station which, he was famous for noting, stood facing the Emperor's palace. The Emperor and the distant people needed to be in direct communication. Yanagita believed folk-tales had always served as the substance and the means of this communication, 'Sanshô' being a prime example. Yanagita and Mizoguchi employ Western technology (anthropology and cinema respectively) to broadcast back to the capital a story whose endearing character comes from its homely origins in the far edges of the world.

Always pious before the past, Mizoguchi made at least a pretence of historical research, given the production schedule.[36] Details of gesture, garments, architecture, traits of geography and class are evident in the hats, boats, temple doors, artisanal objects and landscape. Such fussy effort could amount to an effete, academic antiquarianism if the 'difference' displayed in the distinctive texture of this Japanese past did not contribute to 'Transfiguring Japan'. This is the title of a chapter in Marilyn Ivy's *Discourses of the Vanishing*, devoted to the post-war revival of travel narratives like *Sanshô Dayû*. While a conscious effort to 'discover' and 'exoticise' the land flourished during the 70s and 80s as *Nihonjinron* (pious study of Japan), this impulse had sprung up as soon as the American controls were removed and had roots in the Japanese 'exceptionalism' of the 30s.[37] With nationalism in mind, this family odyssey film plots a map of the archipelago. From Mutsu province in the far northeast, the father is exiled to the southern island of Tsukushi. Meanwhile the rest of the family is intercepted in their trip along the coast of the Sea of Japan, the children enslaved in the Tango prefecture (remote enough from Kyoto to be ruled by a functionary of a corrupt minister), while their mother is marooned on Sado, an island that may stand for the most outlying members of the national body. While the story renders the nation spatially, a temporal axis is staked out in the prologue where the film is explicitly taken to be the most recent of versions that have been passed down through the centuries, thereby compressing Japanese history in the process. One of the first post-Occupation films to figure Japan geographically and historically, *Sanshô Dayû* must be considered a national epic or anthem.

This anthem is doleful, keyed by the cry of Tamaki from the top of the cliff overlooking the sea. 'Zushiô-oo, Anju-uu,' she calls, a mother bird, tethered and bereft of her fledglings. The camera observes her from a high angle, as, leaning on a stick, she hobbles along the bluff following the direction of her cry. We sense her entire body strain to cross the sea with the sounds she sings; we sense it because an offshore wind blows her unbound hair across her cheeks and toward her children. Anju feels her mother's presence come to her through the guarded gates of the

Tamaki's cry blows across Japan

compound. The maternal call, emanating from a most distant and rugged corner, reaches and silently sustains her.

Surely Mizoguchi meant his film to blow across the nation, carrying a mother's cry so as to reawaken in those who hearken to it a memory of belonging to a 'family' that exile (or war) has cruelly dispersed. The cumbersome mechanism of the cinematic apparatus is given over to recovering this pure plaintive cry. It records, amplifies and broadcasts the nearly inaudible echo of a legend that scholars believe had historical origins in the declining years of the Heian period when absentee landlords, virtually independent of government, ruled domains and workhouses overseen by their bailiffs. The earliest extant mention of this tale of slavery and liberation dates from the fourteenth century in the form of a Buddhist homily (soon comprising both a canonical version and a popular 'travelling' tale recited by mendicant priests).[38] During the Tokugawa period Sanshô, Anju and Zushiô were featured in plays produced on both the kabuki and bunraku stages, especially the latter. Then in 1915, Mori Ôgai, among the most famous writers in the land, reworked the *sekkyô-bushi* (Buddhist homily), effectively stabilising it with his rigorous prose, and warping it with his Confucian sentiments. Known for his clarity and naturalism, in this story Ôgai ventured toward a spiritual zone beyond the social where 'the slight aura of mystery surrounding the story permitted him to expand his imagination to an unusual level of sustained lyric sensibility'.[39]

Mizoguchi would be drawn into this zone and would wherever possible inflate Ôgai's spiritual atmosphere, wringing from it a far more tragic tone. Take Anju's suicide. Ôgai narrates it with characteristic obliquity: 'a party of pursuers dispatched by Sanshô the Bailiff in search of Anju and Zushiô ... found a pair of small straw shoes on the shore of the lake below the slope. The shoes were Anju's and she could not be found.' Mizoguchi, at once more direct and more suggestive, watches Anju wade slowly but resolutely into the lake; then, after a cutaway to a faithful friend praying before this pathetic scene, he comes back with a closer shot of the lake, now empty and still, but for the concentric ripples that radiate from a void in the centre. In this, as in so many other scenes, Mizoguchi retained or slightly modified the characters and incidents portrayed by Ôgai, who had done the same – though far more freely – with the anonymous sources he had drawn upon.

Such is the nature of adaptation, and such are the uses of legends. What makes this one memorable is Mizoguchi's focus on the legendary itself, that is, on memory and story-telling. In the first sequence as in the last, the mother practises and demands of her son a discipline of memorisation. Both times she and Zushiô recall and effectively legendise the absent father and his literally unforgettable words. When the mother, Tamaki, is herself lost to the children, her sad tale reaches them (and us) by means of a slave-girl, newly arrived at Sanshô's compound from Sado. Spinning thread as she hums the mother's lament, she may as well be spinning the legend that winds down to us today. Anju questions her excitedly about the origin of the song and Mizoguchi obliges by showing us the terrible moment when Tamaki, having been caught in another escape attempt, has the tendons on her ankles severed. The lament she sings across the Japan Sea has become a pathetic legend on the isle. It constitutes mother's counterpart to father's teaching; it reaches the heart of Anju and eventually of Zushiô when, mystically, they hear it in the forest.

And so, father and mother, from their remote but geographically opposite exiles, exert on their kidnapped children the claims of worlds from which all humans live in exile. Father's claim comes in the shape of the Bodhisattva that Zushiô wears around his neck, a physical sign of civility, a synecdoche of humane social order, founded on the spoken law. Possession of the father's amulet establishes Zushiô's lineage, returning the family to legitimacy when the authorities in Kyoto recognise it. Its powers are social rather than divine, despite its religious meaning.[40] These powers, however, would remain dormant if not activated by the

An itinerant Buddhist preaches a sad tale to peasants (ca. 1620)

spirit carried in the mother's voice. For mother's claim comes not as a physical object but as an intimate symptom, an emanation from her person, calling them to some immaterial place. Her cry is heard first when the children cut branches for shelter on their journey together, then heard again (by Anju only) through the slave-girl; it is heard once more in the burial grove outside the compound. Possessed by the voice, the children are spiritually elevated, prepared to pass through the stages of a journey

Mother and son meet on the other side of hope (production still)

of dispossession that leads them back by different routes to the mother of us all. Anju sinks unnoticed into the lake, while Zushiô moves through temple to palace, acquiring a name and a high social position that he just as quickly discards in his final journey to the mother.[41] He embraces her blindness and anonymity. In the final scene Tamaki's voice has become so immaterial that it emerges from her ragged body without any movement of lips. The film concludes as a cry issuing from the 'Buddhist heart', as one critic called it,[42] beyond all personhood.

When in medieval times the tale was told by wandering priests to indigent peasants, its Buddhist message was meant for a dispossessed people who could identify with the characters or with their plight. Prominent among the tellers were *itako*, blind mendicant women – mediums really – through whose voices were uttered the words of lost souls. Their renditions of Tamaki's final state must have been especially compelling. Imagining them, we can see how the conditions and the moral of this tale of the downtrodden were enacted in the very performing of it. Thus the legend of Sanshô the Bailiff becomes in turn a sacred possession, the passing down of which constitutes the lineage of culture.

Such grass-roots diffusion of the folk-tale persists this century: repeated by teachers in school, the adventures of Anju and Zushiô were included in a popular monthly children's book series; stagings of 'Sanshô' are common even today in Japan,[43] including an opera; certain hotels and inns even advertise their proximity to memorials for the siblings.[44] But Mizoguchi, while ever engaging populist topics, was no mendicant singer. Striving for a more cultured reception, he aimed to perfect the casual ongoingness of the folk-tale. Hence he based his work on Ôgai's beautiful text, not on popular sources. The 'simplicity' that so many French critics praised in his *mise en scène* constitutes not a peasant but a 'refined' presentation, a 'royal value … one of the purest that the cinema has ever given us' where, 'stripped of all contingency, the world appears in its first beauty'.[45] Indeed the film is 'perfect' in the grammatical sense of the term. It aims to perfect the legend, to make it timeless, to display it once and for all, rather than again and again. Mizoguchi hardly took himself to be just another story-teller toiling for the film industry. He was notoriously elitist. Indeed his film seems to want to supplant the legend it passes on, so that 'The Story of Sanshô' continues to our day less through multiple retellings or competing versions than through reactions to this master text. The *legend* and the *legendary* work at cross-purposes.

This paradox of the 'perfected legend' is figured in the film's visual design, through the opposed compositional motifs of line and circle. Dynamic diagonal lines dominate the *mise en scène* and imply succession, perpetuation, lineage and ongoingness; but certain key moments conclude with satisfying circular framings that convey finality and timelessness. The rhythm of the film derives from alternating these looks so that the action, impelled forward, often recklessly, settles into contemplative poses. Anyone familiar with Mizoguchi's *œuvre* will recognise this interplay of diagonals that lead off-screen and more rounded compositions that are contained by the frame. Melodramatic subject matter, soft and malleable, can be readily shaped by a homologous pattern of narration. Indeed, in its etymological sense, melodrama is a name for this pattern, with 'drama' tending to fly beyond the stage in pursuit, while 'melos' makes present the feelings of the story, right there on stage. A common definition of melodrama – that it is a tale of dispersal and regathering particularly suited to the theme of family – fits *Sanshô Dayû*, among a great many of Mizoguchi's films.

Many registers of expression contribute to strong centrifugal movement. From the outset the story displaces a noble family from its

Opening shot: the family 'crosses over'

once proud seat of constancy. The pilgrimage is rendered in diagonal movements across a screen often bisected (as in the opening shot) by an ominous tree trunk or branch. Trees complicate the composition of many of the scenes, unsettling the action. When that action is not framed obliquely and from above in Mizoguchi's habitual way, the camera will uproot itself and wander with or into the scene, keeping us ever conscious of what is out-of-frame. Off-screen sounds – indelibly in scenes of torture – direct the gaze of onlookers, including that of the spectator. During moments of frantic action, as when a slave is chased down or in the orgy following the liberation of the slaves, the camera frames diagonals and then displaces itself to locate still other oblique angles, contributing to the dynamism of what is represented. Unforgettably in the kidnapping scene, and occasionally elsewhere, Mizoguchi even uses jagged montage to create spatial disequilibrium, each shot calling for a successor, and still another, cascading forward in a *mise en scène* of dispersal.

The pathetic effects of dispersion are multiplied by a couple of Mizoguchi's patented tactics. In the flashback sequences, and again at the court in Kyoto, counterbalanced diagonals suggest the regulated force-field of politics. The character dominating the scene may be in the foreground or seated on a square mat, one corner near the camera, its diagonals radiating out to intersect at acute or oblique angles the many rectilinear beams in the room. Anyone entering such a room is perforce subject to a clearly pre-arranged power structure. Out in the forest, by

The family shelter
infiltrated (production still)

contrast, the context is much harder to read. Not cut beams, but tangled branches frame these scenes and confuse the eye, even when the trees bend in a leading, often foreboding direction. The family, chased from the stability of their ancestral home, will henceforth need to search for shelter. The jerry-rigged campsite made of branches and grass, the false shelter the priestess offers, the hut at the edge of Sanshô's compound, the canopy the siblings make for their dying friend Namiji, and the miserable beach dwelling of the film's finale are all pathetic attempts to recover a home.[46]

Mizoguchi's patented depth of field promotes this *mise en scène* of dispersion. Characters exit away from the spectator, when they slip behind some structure in the rear plane (the failed escape of the aged slave), or disappear in the distance (Tarô and later Zushiô bounding down a winding road that loses itself in the mountains). Figures rush abruptly straight from the camera in pursuit of others to the rear of the screen, pushing the action out into the void beyond what can be seen. All three techniques (diagonal lines, depth of field, front to rear motion) are brilliantly deployed in the film's most wrenching moment, the kidnapping on the shore not far from the port of Naoe.

The sequence opens with the family led by the false priestess walking toward the camera, then diagonally off-screen right. A medium shot finds two villains looking back at the group, licking their chops in anticipation of easy prey. The screen is bisected by a beached boat pointing diagonally out to the empty sea. A dozen shots now follow. An ominous tree ushers the unsuspecting family toward their destiny at the boats. As

soon as the last of them nearly reaches the edge of the screen on the right, they march on the opposite diagonal following the kidnappers to the boats. A static group shot of the family and duplicitous priestess maintains a line that crosses from bottom right to upper left, while the boatmen carry supplies horizontally across the top of the screen behind them. One man interrupts the group, grabbing Tamaki and pulling her away. The camera pans to isolate her being escorted into the boat, along the same diagonal line. She turns back to the shore, a flicker of suspicion crossing her face. The reverse shot from her point of view shows her family and the bandits clustered theatrically as the nurse prepares to join her. This static moment erupts when a bandit pushes the nurse directly at the camera and onto the boat, which is already moving away from shore with the camera aboard. Simultaneously the children are pulled up the shore by the priestess, doubling the separation on the vertical axis of the screen. Frantic, Tamaki and the nurse plead with the boatmen who pole the boat diagonally up to the right, while a cut shows the children from below as they futilely struggle. A long shot now includes both groups: the boat in the far plane moves along the diagonal of the bay while the children rush into the bottom left of the screen crying 'Mother, mother,' and run along the shore gaining only slightly on the escaping boat. The camera waits briefly, then follows the diagonal line at its own pace. In this way, three distinct movements (boat, children, camera) flow slightly out of synchronisation along the shore toward the open sea. The next pair of shots isolates the two groups, putting them graphically at odds. The boat is poled from the foreground up the screen's vertical axis away from the camera while Tamaki and the nurse struggle and desperately plead with their captors. Cut to a rare horizontal composition as the children in extreme long shot run along a spit of shore screaming their distress and being restrained by the other kidnapper. A shot from the boat includes both groups again, Tamaki being pushed away in the foreground while the children are momentarily visible on the shore being pulled back. But the boat drifts diagonally left and the camera pans with it, losing the children in the process. A reverse shot from behind the children shows the boat in the distant plane while the children run into the water away from the camera toward it. A cut on the same axis but ahead of the children isolates the boat now further out at sea. The camera remains utterly still even when the nurse goes overboard, waves her arms and sinks. The desperate cries of Tamaki and her children cue the wail of a high-pitched flute, and the sequence fades out with the boat small and suspended in the centre of a monochromatic grey field of surrounding water.

A similar stylistic economy can be felt in Mori Ôgai's rendition of the same scene. He has one of the kidnappers taunt the distraught mother whom he is rowing away from her children with the aphorism: 'Any boat you board is the ship of the Buddha, bound for the same Other Shore.' Without elaboration Ôgai continues:

> Mad with grief, [she] pulled herself up as far as she could on the gunwales of the boat. She called to the children, 'the worst fate has befallen us. We may never see each other again. Anju, always take care of your guardian amulet, the image of Jizô, your guardian god … and always do your best to keep together.' The children could do nothing more than call hopelessly for their mother. The boats drew farther and farther apart. The children's mouths seemed to stay open like young birds waiting for their food, but their cries no longer could traverse the widening distance.[47]

Ôgai has lengthened and deepened this scene which is already prominent in the ancient Buddhist source text. There, much more matter-of-factly, we hear the mother plead with her children as they are taken off in the opposite direction:

> 'Take good care of the image of Jizô bosatsu. It may act as a substitute for your lives. Brother, hold on to the family scroll. If you die show it to Emma-o. You will be treated better.' But the mother's voice doesn't reach the other boat anymore. So she takes her fan and begins to wave to her children.[48]

The film dramatises the separation physically. The wail of a flute takes over for the diminishing cries of the children after the nurse has gone under; then Tamaki in extreme long shot is shown overcome and dragged down into the boat. Measuring the unbridgeable distance that yawns between mother and children is a mercilessly unmoving camera. Thus as a kind of compensation, this traumatic sequence of violent dispersion comes to rest on a timeless, even beautiful image of metaphysical isolation. Mizoguchi distributes the feeling of this wrenching farewell across the entirety of his film; yet the final shot in the sequence

Buddhist statue, the rounded sublimate of Anju's watery death

manages to contain this agony, lifting it to a higher aesthetic plane. In this it rhymes with Anju's suicide in the pool of water, a tableau that is paradigmatic of the film's opposite, inward movement, its *mise en scène* of gathering.

Anju's suicide sublimates pain into exquisite eternal calm. Her companion looks off-screen at this holy sacrifice, praying just inside a gate that is swung open, a gate to the other world.[49] What she sees are the concentric circles spreading out from the point of Anju's disappearance, framed by arching branches that complete an oval begun by the rounded shoreline. An elegiac dissolve performs the spiritual metamorphosis of Anju to a higher level, by matching the circle of the lake to the form of a Buddha in the temple where Zushiô has sought cover. This Buddha, stately before us in a moment of rare frontal symmetry, may represent the director, Mizoguchi Kenji, calmly overlooking the suffering and frantic activity that dart by diagonally from all directions. In the famous finale he will crane away from his characters to frame the impersonal seascape where one can glimpse in the foreground the seaweed gatherer going about his unending task. The beach in this case, like the sea and the pond in the earlier shots, becomes a background of indifference that swallows human gestures. The beach and bay, framed by dark silhouettes of land masses, looking like great whales, outlast history. The human drama dwindles beneath a setting that overwhelms all differences in a primal homogeneity.

Where the diagonal leads the camera and the spectator beyond the frame in a line-of-flight that makes the present moment find its reason in the next moment, the circle suggests the stability and self-sufficiency of return and 'gathering'. This sensibility, triumphant at the end, predominates also in the film's first act, before the violence of the kidnapping breaks the delicate ambiance into shards. In the opening sequence, the family moves tentatively forward along a line that they expect will ultimately describe a family circle, coming back to father whose exile started the movement in the first place. Lengthy dissolves switch the image three times into flashbacks of the father before returning each time to the travellers who meanwhile have moved forward in their journey toward him. These dissolves stitch distant people and times into a single image and they unite mother and son in their collective memory. It is the son who asks his mother about father, then races away from the camera down the forest path. A match dissolve tracks the child Zushiô running amid the general frenzy at the family's manor as the military officer and his men demand the father's departure. Inside, seated ceremonially on a mat, the father defends his actions until the camera drifts down to settle on Tamaki, witnessing the proceedings; she bows her head in resignation. A dissolve returns us to Tamaki by a forest stream, dipping a bowl and bringing water to the family group that gathers around a campfire. Once again Mizoguchi's camera moves off the centred action to float to Tamaki as she lifts the rounded bowl to her lips conjuring up her husband again who, for a few seconds, shares the screen with her, drinking from a bowl himself. In this flashback the father gives the sacred heirloom to the child Zushiô who repeats the father's teachings, until another dissolve returns us not to the

Memory unites Tamaki and her husband

mother, as it should, but to the adolescent Zushiô still reciting the mantra and holding the Bodhisattva that is securely tied around his neck. He thus has shared this memory of his father with Tamaki to whom the camera next glides as the group continues along the trail. When the flashbacks have done their work and the father has been sent in one direction, his family in another, one more dissolve brings us to a magnificent profile of Tanaka Kinuyo. Her aristocratic oval hat, an *ichime gasa*, forms an umbrella over the top half of the screen, protecting the memories in her mind and the children visible in the middle plane on the shore. Tamaki calls them to her, and together they walk through a sea of tall grass, stately *susuki*, that waves in the autumn breeze, and engulfs them protectively. The mother will attempt to build a shelter that night, a

Authentic period hat
ichime gasa shelters
Tamaki's memories

canopy of branches and grass against the elements and evil spirits that threaten her children from off-screen.

Mizoguchi generates pathos by intersecting the fullness of circles with sharp secants, then retreating so as to contain all lines in a comprehensive arc. In one exceptional moment these two geometrical figures fuse as a metaphor of cinema itself. When the new slave-girl is brought in from Sado Island, Anju trains her to wind thread. The thread represents the continuity of the song she sings, of the legend attached to it, and thus of the lineage of culture. But the winding – and in particular the reels onto which the thread is wound – ought then to be taken as the film projector unspooling the very story we are watching. This would be a figure of the film in its perfect tense, visible all at once before us, though released frame by frame in projection.

While circular motifs (the ancient stones that open the film, the spools of thread, the Buddha) and circular compositions directly present values that have been gathered for contemplation, certain editing patterns carry out the action of gathering. The clearest of these are the dissolves by which the mother is shown to call the past into the present. When the children are out gathering branches and long grass they hear (and in a cutaway we see) their mother call them from screen right. Anju hearkens, turning to face her mother's voice. Zushiô claims not to hear, but then follows his sister. This simple pattern of cry and response, built on a standard editing design, will be elaborated in the central sequence where the mother's cry reaches Anju from across the Japan Sea. In the film's most mystical moment, Anju speaks to Zushiô of their mother, then hears an echo of her voice. Zushiô at first hears nothing, but accepts his mother's presence and determines on the spot to escape. This turning point answers, in a single shot, the break-up of the family near the port of Naoe figured in those dozen violently juxtaposed shots. Importantly, the scene in the forest carries two sounds, that of the echo of the mother's voice and, almost subliminally, the call of a wood pigeon. Mizoguchi here permits the naturalisation of a miracle: Anju, having recalled to her brother the

Twice the siblings frolic, then hearken to mother's spirit

moment when as children they had heard their mother's cry, transforms the bird sounds into that cry. She fills out her present with an absence that also affects her brother. Sound, like the aura of the mother, is able to float from off-screen, across sharp breaks in the visual field, to suffuse those who sense it.

The children's sense of their mother's out-of-field presence sustains a yearning for a higher union beyond the exile of earthly life. In certain moments, a great metaphysical circuit is implied within a single shot, wherein the characters are answered by an off-screen presence vaguely felt. When, still pondering her husband, Tamaki carries a bowl of water to Anju at the campfire, a thin wisp of smoke from the fire floats like incense to disappear toward the top of the screen. In rising into the atmosphere, the smoke forms a conduit from the family to the invisible. The high angle of the camera might be thought to represent the perspective of the cosmos, watching with care the anxious group whose campfire constitutes a holy offering. This shot can be related to the finale of *Ugetsu*, with the smoke of the offering at Miyagi's grave lifting the camera literally to a higher plane of vision. A similar movement in spiritual level concludes *Sanshô Dayû* as well, when the camera, in looking away from the remnant of the family, is said to interrogate an uncaring cosmos. This time the cosmos seems not to look back on Tamaki and Zushiô who have nothing left to offer. Denuded, they huddle without desire or prayer, mere bodies who accept the state of things. Zushiô has given up his pretence to governing, and has thereby released himself and us from all cares. The circuit that he has made – to father's grave, to Anju's pond and to mother's beach – expands to the vast circle of the universe which gathers all bodies without distinction. The metaphysical vision, Buddhist in character, of the famous concluding shots of *Sanshô Dayû* and *Ugetsu* have established Mizoguchi as an auteur in the West, indeed as a 'Master'. These tableaux that drift from the featured characters to frame anonymous peasants in the distance have left

Final shot: oblivious seaweed-gatherers on the oblivious shore

viewers filled with an unnamable emotion. The peasants are oblivious of the drama and of the camera. They gather their seaweed or grain, while in each case the line of the shot stretches far beyond them as the crane lifts our eyes beyond all drama, where the act of gathering transcends the family, and where care becomes disinterested and care-less.

Mizoguchi, Bailiff of Culture

The cosmic perspective Mizoguchi reaches in the film's finale has had the effect of lifting it from its remote mountain origins and making it available to audiences everywhere. His high art rendition of what was originally a homespun tale flourished in an international marketplace hungry for moral melodramas. The year 1954 set a high watermark for the tides of humanist discourse that sloshed around the globe. Expressions from Japan were particularly valued because this country had caused incalculable anguish throughout the Eastern Hemisphere and had in turn been punished by a vicious atomic attack. Films like Kurosawa's *Rashômon* (1950) and *Ikiru* (1952), followed at the end of the decade by superproductions such as Kobayashi's *The Human Condition* (1959), surprised the West with the maturity of their subject matter. In this context *Sanshô Dayû* delivered its deadly serious message in a tone of august profundity.

'Universal humanism' might well be a modern invention; in any case, after the disaster of nationalism, it emerged as a central post-war theme. No less an authority than Jean-Paul Sartre proclaimed it so in his 1946 clarion pamphlet 'Existentialism is a Humanism'. In December 1948 the infant United Nations voted in its 'Universal Declaration of Human Rights', vowing to guarantee the sanctity of the individual against political oppression.

In synchrony with the optimism of the moment, and just before the cold war trenches were dug, international film festivals promulgated the 'unity of mankind'. 1946 saw Cannes mount its first great festival and award a 'peace prize' to the film that best fostered universal human understanding.[50] Venice, scrubbing away a fascist past, re-established itself the following spring as the most serious of the festivals. It featured a retrospective of international silent classics and championed new works coming from Mexico, Czechoslovakia, Denmark, India and Sweden. For the first time since the overblown prophecies of D.W. Griffith and Abel Gance, cinema was officially proclaimed the medium of cross-cultural understanding. The Venice festival declared itself 'a token of international cooperation based on common ideals of art and culture ... [and] a token of the solidarity among peoples who at bottom wish to understand one another and are anxious to be friends'.[51] The cinema, it was alleged, transformed human suffering and aspirations into narrative and pictorial art for the whole world to experience together. With intellectuals turning to the medium (Sartre wrote, then repudiated, *Les Orgueilleux* which screened at the 1953 Venice festival), the post-war cinema appeared to share with literature the task of exploring the human predicament. Indeed cinema was thought to have an edge on literature because of its potential for global distribution, for mass spectatorship, and above all for the kind of cultural reciprocity evident at the festivals. There, films from Mexico really did stand up to those from Great Britain, assured of attention from producers, directors and critics who gathered from around the world to gauge the progress of the art each year.

Into this environment came, unannounced, the astonishing *Rashômon*, triumphant at Venice in the spring of 1951. It would be followed in successive years by Mizoguchi's *The Life of Oharu* (1952), *Ugetsu* and *Sanshô Dayû*, and by Kurosawa's *Seven Samurai* (1954), all of them winning the 'Golden Lion'. Meanwhile Cannes too discovered Japan, awarding its grand prize in 1954 to *Gate of Hell*. After a half-century of virtual invisibility in the West,[52] Japanese cinema suddenly vaulted to the summit of critical acclaim.

Rashômon's reputation – modest at home, until its apotheosis in Europe – has become a saga nearly as well known as the film. With hindsight, one can recognise that *Rashômon* contained the ingredients that would please festival audiences. Concluding sentimentally on the cry of an abandoned baby, it audaciously thrust a rape at its centre, and then, via contradictory flashbacks, questioned society's ability to comprehend the atrocity, or to reset its moral equilibrium through justice and retribution. Its multiple perspectives reminded educated audiences of William Faulkner or of *Citizen Kane*. Indeed *Rashômon* intimated that Japan might have secretly attained a vanguard position in the kind of modern cinema inaugurated by Orson Welles.[53] On the basis of this single example, Kurosawa had instantly entered critical discourse as an auteur, a film-maker in control of his subject and his medium, whose style proposed a significant view of the world, one that would be repeated with variations in subsequent works.

Allegedly Mizoguchi was chagrined that his younger colleague had been honoured in the West before him. Their rivalry played itself out each year in the festival circuit up to Mizoguchi's death. For all that, *Sanshô Dayû* in fact shares a number of features with *Rashômon*, enough to suggest that Daiei Studios financed *Sanshô Dayû* because of their windfall with the Kurosawa film. Both films derive from prominent writers of the early Taishô period, who had themselves turned to ancient folk material from the late Heian period for their plots. In this way, both films carry within them not just an individual style, but a millennium of Japanese culture. Still, it was as auteurs rather than cultural transmitters that both film-makers were lionised. Like *Rashômon*, *Sanshô Dayû* contains flashbacks; it too represents extremes of cruelty and selflessness, meditating outright in certain scenes on the general plight and moral constitution of human beings. Its style, in many ways antithetical to that of *Rashômon*, is so distinctive as to constitute a clear vision of the world that critics found themselves able to recognise, to describe, and to compare with other styles, Kurosawa's above all. The critics at *Cahiers du Cinéma* accused Kurosawa of dazzling the spectator through surface effects that had little more to them than an exotic Eastern veneer covering ersatz ideas that were not truly Japanese in their origin or presentation. This criticism annoyed André Bazin, who knew that 'at *Cahiers*, the director of *Rashômon* is somewhat the victim of a prejudice which works to the advantage of the tender, musical Mizoguchi'. But he defended *Ikiru* as a masterpiece because it 'is a specifically Japanese film and … [because of] the universal value of its message. … I still perhaps prefer Mizoguchi's style, like the pure Japanese music of his inspiration, but I surrender before the breadth of intellectual, moral, and aesthetic perspectives opened up by [Kurosawa].'[54]

Jacques Rivette did not surrender to Kurosawa, arguing that in the cinema ideas are less important than the way they are displayed and that the real foreign language one must learn so as to appreciate a film made in Tokyo or Kyoto is not Japanese but the language of *mise en scène*, where Mizoguchi triumphs over the prosaic Kurosawa:

> The little Kurosawa–Mizoguchi game has had its day. Let the latest champions of Kurosawa withdraw from the match; one can only compare what is comparable and equal in ambition. Mizoguchi alone imposes the sense of a specific language and world, answerable only

to him. ... Alone, it seems, of all the Japanese filmmakers to stay within his own traditions ... he is also the only one who can thus lay claim to true universality, which is that of the individual.[55]

Twenty years later, Noël Burch would reverse this judgment, proclaiming Kurosawa the post-war director most committed to a trenchantly modernist *mise en scène*. In his view Mizoguchi (as well as Ozu) had retreated from a strong 30s style to present a watered-down, Eastern poetry, exactly the sort to seduce Bazin, Rivette, Godard and a whole generation.[56]

Whatever the judgment, then or now, Mizoguchi confronted issues paramount to Western intellectuals during the cold war, particularly the *universality* of human values, and the distinctiveness of *individual* perspective. An elite audience in the West was primed to take Mizoguchi as a kind of spiritual emissary whose delicate 'musical' sensibility, having been put through the hell of wartime Japan, was capable of registering and expressing feelings of degradation and hope the rest of us could scarcely imagine. Indeed, *Sanshô Dayû*'s themes of exile and slavery resonate even more strongly today in a world where human rights violations have become epidemic. Terrence Malick intimated that the subject matter of 'Sanshô', children in the clutches of a tyrant, drew him because of its universality. He came to it in fact on a rebound, when in 1992 he was forced to scuttle another stage adaptation, also about vulnerable siblings kidnapped and tortured, 'Hansel and Gretel'. 'Sanshô the Bailiff' had the advantage for Malick of its Asian origin and Buddhist halo, and to ensure a 'cross-cultural' effect he engaged André Wajda, the great Polish cineaste, to direct his adaptation for its scheduled Broadway run.[57] Wajda promised 'to create something that seems like Japanese theater, but isn't', underscored by a 'blend of Japanese and European orchestration'.[58]

And so *Sanshô Dayû*'s producer Masaichi Nagata had been on the mark when he banked on the growth of internationalist sentiment in the West. This was his fourth success in a row for Daiei Studios at Venice, and he was honoured by the Japanese government at the end of 1954 for making the culture known abroad and opening up new avenues of export. In fact, however, despite its decorations, *Sanshô Dayû* made virtually no money at European or American box offices, at least not until its re-release years later. At home it played to 70,000 spectators in its first two weeks at three Tokyo theatres. This was a respectable showing at best. Chosen ninth in the *Kinema Junpô* annual list of top films, *Sanshô Dayû* was bested by Kinoshita's *Twenty-Four Eyes*, Kurosawa's *Seven Samurai*, and his own *Tale of the Crucified Lovers*, the Mizoguchi film many Japanese connoisseurs have since held up as his most Japanese and his best. Indeed one champion of *Tale of the Crucified Lovers* explicitly preferred it to *Sanshô Dayû* which he felt was compromised by its overt appeal to Western intellectuals.[59]

This critic may have had in mind the coincidence of *Sanshô Dayû*'s democratic message with the American Occupation's programme for democratising Japan. Perhaps to counter the West's patronising and missionary attitude, Mizoguchi meant to reclaim for Japan a native strain of humanism that goes back to medieval times. In any case, one cannot deny the universality of the father's dictum, 'all men are born equal in the world and all have a right to happiness.' Nor can one deny the equally universal impulse to doubt the foundation of such claims, since *Sanshô Dayû* tests the virtuous family *à la* Job, and questions both the evil order of the universe and the power of men to act morally within it.[60]

'Evil' extends far beyond the film's title character. It contaminates government (the greedy, lecherous emissary of the Minister of the Right) and religion (the false Shinto priestess); and it permeates society in the undiluted poison of slavery.[61] Slavery seems the very state of nature, for it pre-dates Zushiô's father, who is exiled for refusing to turn over the peasants in his province to the generals for their wars. His failed action stands out in a system to which all are enslaved. Down the ladder of power, all are branded, some literally like cattle. The Bailiff, then, incarnates not just evil but its banality, for he routinely passes down a norm of action. Overseer, headman, he is the local official and doing, he is told, a terrific job. To break this chain of iniquity, Tarô renounces power altogether and the social system built upon it. Zushiô will copy him by climbing off his horse and taking the boat to Sado Island where he approaches his mother having reached her state of dispossession.

Moral readings of *Sanshô Dayû* lead swiftly to allegorical interpretation. Condoning resistance to generals (those who order conscripted soldiers to attack their neighbours or those who occupy one's land), Mizoguchi never goes so far as to question the seat of authority itself. The Emperor remains unblemished in this film and in Japan, no matter how corrupt his ministers may be. Mizoguchi follows Ôgai in situating the drama in the late eleventh century, when the Emperor was 'protected' from all but symbolic responsibilities. But symbols prove important, for it was the Emperor who originally gave the heirloom to Zushiô's father. Passed down thereafter, paradoxically it represents paternity, the sanctity of which is lodged in the Emperor, as much as the equality of human beings. Mizoguchi's film – indeed the man himself – was caught in this paradox.

Civilisation and barbarism co-exist in every period but seldom in so openly extreme a manner as in the time of *Sanshô*. The atrocities recounted in the legend occurred as the Heian era, usually mentioned for the supreme refinement of its court life, degenerated into lawlessness, most certainly for commoners. Life in Sanshô's compound was unspeakably brutal, yet Zushiô's father embodies principles that fit his gentlemanly demeanour and apparel. His wife, elegant even in the forest, knows just how to hold a cup in her hands. The children are well mannered. And so one may question whether Mizoguchi tells of the birth of civilisation or quite the opposite, the fall of an aristocratic family from a graceful life into chaos. A Marxist critic lamented the film's attention to the pathos of the well-born rather than to strategies that might oppose the exploitation of masses of slaves.[62]

When Zushiô frees the slaves, he understands that his gesture can only temporarily interrupt a system that is as pervasive as it is nefarious. More troubling, this local liberation, as far as the film is concerned, produces not benevolence but a drunken orgy and a fire that destroys the entire compound. Some of those who stagger about the bonfire so wildly had earlier, upon command, performed a delicate formal dance for the

Corruption within civilisation

envoy of the Minister of the Right. Does barbarism produce art, while freedom returns humans to a crude state of nature? For his part, Zushiô abandons the people to their own devices; indeed he abandons civilisation altogether to reunite with his mother in an embrace out of the reach of the social. On a forgotten spit of beach, under a darkening, uncaring sky, mother and son do not look forward to a better world. They look forward precisely to nothing.

This Buddhist conclusion to the film seems at odds with the Buddhist parable it relays. For in the oldest extant version, Zushiô discovers both father and mother alive; together they build a monument to Anju whose spirit has entered the Jizô statue that looked after her. Civilisation henceforth issues from the righteous family protected by the divinity of one of its own. But for Mizoguchi slavery is not so readily overcome. It is endemic to civilisation, evident in orders coming down from wartime and occupation generals, as well as in those coming from producers. Mizoguchi himself exacted obedience, labour and pain from those under him. Stories abound. He ordered innumerable script revisions and countless repetitions in rehearsal, never praising his exhausted cast and crew. He put Tanaka Kinuyo on a meagre diet for weeks before the shooting of the final sequence, just to intensify her miserable appearance. Mizoguchi was a tryant or, perhaps worse, a bailiff.

And whom did he serve if not the civilisation of Japan, to whose literature and art he was devoted and which in turn sustained his career? In the case of *Sanshô Dayû*, the prestige of Ôgai's story largely tied his hands. Ôgai himself had complained of being chained to the tale while writing it.[63] Both of these artists stood in a line of command whose summit recedes into the mist of the past. Because of his lack of formal education, Mizoguchi retained an inordinate admiration for traditional culture and a respect for those at home within it. As enslaving as tradition may have been, did he want to see it burned to the ground in an orgy of freedom? Did he want to live among those liberated slaves who would dance around the pyre to wild rhythms (the youth culture enamoured of American values)? Mizoguchi's art depends on, and profits from, servitude to cultural heritage; and particularly in the later films his humanism advances inhumanely. To break the system one would have to renounce the value of tradition altogether, as Zushiô does, renouncing in effect the value of 'value' so that there would be nothing worth overseeing, no cultural goods worth fabricating, lording over and passing down.

Mizoguchi may have entertained such anarchic notions but certainly did not hold them. He and Zushiô both follow the stream of tradition that leads to magnificent gardens of culture – first to the temple and then to the palace in Kyoto. This stream, however, flows past the culture it waters, down to a forlorn delta where it empties into the sea. The uplifting Confucianism of Mori Ôgai's parable sinks like water into the sand on the beach where the film deposits Zushiô. It has been argued that Mizoguchi surely wanted to deliver a children's tale raised to the level of adult education, a civic homily about human rights and behaviour, whose tone and sentiments come straight from the mouth of the father;[64] but the film took a darker turn. The father disappears and Zushiô forsakes civilisation, crossing the sea 'on the ship of the Buddha, bound for the same Other Shore'. There, on the hither side of history, out of earshot even of the seaweed gatherer, he finds his mother moaning in the face of the nothingness to which her family has been brought.

This negative theology carries a Buddhist pedigree, which accounts in some measure for its attractiveness to the educated audiences of film festivals and art houses of the 50s.[65] Jean-Luc Godard signalled just this when he hailed Mizoguchi as uniquely able to 'to describe an adventure, which is at the same time a cosmogony',[66] and Lindsay Anderson identified that cosmogony with the Zen Buddhism that Alan Watts was making fashionable in England at the time.[67] This context is important to the reception of *Sanshô Dayû*. For, while the importance of Zen to Japanese Buddhism has been greatly over-emphasised, and while the film's clear Buddhist sympathies lie with the Jôdo sect, as Carole Cavanaugh demonstrates, a Western obsession with Zen had been born from the meeting of a post-war (existentialist) spiritual crisis and the simultaneous re-discovery of Japan. Updated editions of classic Zen commentaries by Daisetz Suzuki and Nyogen Senzaki were followed in 1949 by a popular handbook by Christmas Humphreys, a prominent British diplomat devoted to Suzuki. Humphreys introduced the aged Suzuki to his young disciple Alan Watts resulting in new books by all three men along with Suzuki's collected essays. *Sanshô Dayû* was released in Paris at the same time as French translations of Watts and of a key book by David Linnson. These supplemented Hubert Benoit's classic *Le Doctrine suprême* (1953) whose English version had been generously introduced by Aldous Huxley.

These specialised books anchored the more vulgar brand of Zen purveyed by the American beat writers (Jack Kerouac, Gary Snyder, Allen Ginsberg), and by the café philosophers in Paris who recognised Zen's kinship with an existentialism then at its peak. As for the artworld, *Zen in the Fifties*[68] documents the saturation of Paris galleries with *neo-japonisme*, involving Pierre Alechinsky, Jean Degottex and most prominent, Yves Klein. In comparison to the English and the Germans, the French may have been less drawn to the philosophical substrate of Zen, but they were fascinated by its manifestations in flower arranging, tea ceremony and calligraphy. Eugene Herrigel's bestseller, *Zen and Archery*, written in German, was translated into French immediately in 1953. It bore illustrations by Georges Braque, who was smitten by Zen.[69]

In such a milieu, the contemplative indifference on which *Sanshô Dayû* ends appears as a moral achievement over suffering. Western spectators could compare this achievement to that of, say, Joseph Conrad or André Malraux whose novels are often set beyond the pale of morality and whose heroes – over-reachers, idealists, revolutionaries (Lord Jim, for instance, or Garine, in *Les Conquerants*) – wind up on the other side of despair where the significance of their lofty missions shrivels.[70]

Conclusion

In his final books, philosopher Jean-François Lyotard came to attribute this sort of inhuman humanism to André Malraux. The heroes of Malraux's novels (Garine, or Kyo in *Man's Fate*) risk everything for world-shattering revolutions; however, they act without believing in victory, expending themselves and sacrificing others in grand gestures of abandonment. Malraux may promulgate insubordination to colonisation as did Mizoguchi to slavery, but their sermons die out in diminishing echoes, leaving only a frozen silence in the presence of things. Lyotard put his finger on a citation from Malraux that resonates with *Sanshô Dayû*: 'Little does it matter that humans pass down for a few centuries their ideas and their techniques: for humans are nothing but a happenstance; what is essential is a world made of oblivion.'[71] Malraux situates himself in a domain 'before the birth of the gods, anterior to religion', where something like an 'I without me' speaks and listens. This hovering state of being before (or after) history, religion and personhood – which Mizoguchi seems also or differently to have reached – is what Westerners gropingly mean by 'Zen'. This achievement of spiritual

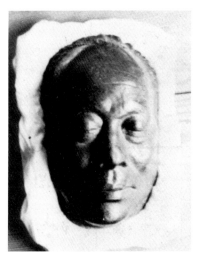

discipline, this space of knowledge carved out by art rather than thought, comes by way of the slight discrepancy between what one hears while one speaks and what others hear. When Anju in the forest 'hears' her mother, while speaking of her to Zushiô, she is actually listening to the sound of her own voice within herself, while the audience hears an echo produced by a technical modulation in the soundtrack. Lyotard would say that Anju hears her own self speaking in her throat, her throat in fact listening to an echo that resounds in the 'muffled chamber' of her body. Mizoguchi finds the universe itself to be such a 'chambre sourde', where works of art resound as interior echoes.

The universe as muffled chamber is inhabited likewise by Orson Welles, that other noble nihilist of cinema's classic era. Recall his Shakespeare films where the Bard's authoritative voice reverberates in diminished tones within the cinema, our century's most authentic way to register what once was so powerfully said. Amounting to mere 'echoes of art', Welles's films still constitute for our times the function that art has served immemorially: to attest to the presence of things, including the 'human thing', beyond mere aspiration.[72]

In just this way *Sanshô Dayû* retells its timeless tale to attest to the empty state of things in a post-war and post-Occupation Japan. In a final

gesture Mizoguchi cranes above history to look out on a future that is hopeless. At such a distance he hears – in the internal echo of a sound emitted in the throat of his film – a call from the past. We give a name to this practice whereby the space of an echo is filled when one listens intently to one's own

Top Deathmask: Mizoguchi as legend
Below Pilgrimage to Mizoguchi: Jean-Luc Godard

71

internal murmur. We call it prayer. Mizoguchi's hopeless prayer lets us sense in the echo of the story of Sanshô, and especially in the call of Tamaki, the hollow body of Japanese culture which will never belong fully to the present, even though its surface may be branded with the grotesque tattoos of modernity.

Terrence Malick, Victor Erice, Jean-Luc Godard and Theo Angelopoulos are among the most illustrious Western film-makers to pass on the legend of Mizoguch Kenjii. An entourage of cinephiles have made the pilgrimage to his grave beside a small temple in Kyoto. The photographs taken there might be placed alongside the shot of the ancient ruins that opens *Sanshô Dayû*, for they are, all of them, pious memorials that testify to a brutal but majestic era, to the precious moral and aesthetic sensibility that grew up in such conditions, and to the passing away of these as of all things.

NOTES

· ·

The version of the film used by the authors in this study is the Criterion laserdisc of 1994. Particularly valuable is the added historical material on the disc which was commissioned by Terence Malick and provided by Geisler/Roberdeau Productions.

1 The location of the ouster that launches the narrative unlocks a political metaphor. Hiraizumi, the seat of regional power in the northeastern province of Mutsu, was for centuries an outpost where the 'civilised' world of Yamato met the 'barbarian' world of the Emishi, who resisted colonisation by the Japanese Imperial centre. Kyoto relied on collaborating Emishi families who were rewarded with court titles and hereditary control over wide territories. Brutal wars among the clans, between 1051 and 1087, ended with the ascendance of the Hiraizumi Fujiwara, a military family regarded by their distant relatives in the capital as barbarians. The Hiraizumi Fujiwara carried on the historical resistance to central Japanese rule but with a splendour that rivalled the Kyoto court. Taira no Masauji, a civilian administrator whose exile in 1081 led to the enslavement of his children under the legendary Sanshô the Bailiff, was no doubt a victim of these political upheavals. Japanese history can be generally understood as a saga of conflict and collaboration between the central Yamato state and powerful military families in the provinces. Masauji's confrontation with local samurai represents centuries of strife between two fundamental Japanese impulses – one courtly and urban, the other military and rustic.
2 Mori Ôgai, 'Rekishi sono mama to rekishi banare', in David Dilworth and J. Thomas Rimer (eds), *The Historical Fiction of Mori Ôgai*, trans. Darcy Murray (Honolulu: University of Hawaii Press, 1991), p. 151.
3 Ibid.
4 The earliest *sekkyô-bushi* (Buddhist parable) source with the title 'Sanshô dayû', a text based on earlier sermons and oral tradition, dates from between 1624 and 1644 ('Sanshô dayû') but this source has several omissions. The earliest complete version was written in 1656 ('Sekkyô Sanshô dayû'). A 1667 source ('Sanshô dayû') is the first to mention that the mother is sold to Sado; in the earlier sources she is sold to Ezokashima. For this reason, Sakô Nobuyuki traces Mori Ôgai's version to the 1667 text. Mori

Ôgai makes several changes in place names and other details as he describes in 'Rekishi sono mama to rekishi banare'. See Sakô Nobuyuki, *Sanshô dayû densetsu no kenkyû* (Tokyo: Meicho shuppan, 1992), pp. 1–4.
5 See Bruno Bettelheim, *The Uses of Enchantment: The Meaning and Importance of Fairy Tales* (New York: Knopf, 1976), p. 37. Bettelheim identifies elements in the genre and stipulates that the genuine fairy-tale must end happily. Precluded then are many of the stories of Hans Christian Anderson (among the European authors Ôgai admired) whose narratives probably constitute a genre transitional to melodrama.
6 The estate administered by Sanshô is a tax-immune *shôen* in Tango, an area in modern-day Kyoto prefecture and, at the time of the story, far from the influence of the capital. The *shôen* were owned by absentee noblemen who lived in Heian-kyô (Kyoto) and who left the administration of their estates to local bailiffs. The prosperity, autonomy and increasing strength of the *shôen* contributed to the collapse of Imperial rule in 1185.
7 The English subtitle translates the Japanese word *yume* (dream) as 'fairy-tale'.
8 Hasegawa Kôhei, *Sanshô dayû to Mori Ôgai*, Bungaku kyôshitsu 3 (Gakuyûsha, 1949), pp. 142–3.
9 Peter Brooks, *The Melodramatic Imagination: Balzac, Henry James, Melodrama and the Mode of Excess* (New Haven: Yale University Press, 1976), p. 5.
10 Yann Tobin points out the moral symbolism of the two fathers in 'Le bruit des vagues', *Positif*, no. 236, November 1980, p. 32.
11 Brooks, *Melodramatic Imagination*, p. 22.
12 The surprise of seeing the children suddenly grown is lost in the subtitled version. An English inter-title over the foundation stones tells us that a decade has gone by and the children are adults. I have seen only the subtitled version of the film but I assume that the original did not contain an explanatory inter-title in Japanese.

13 Stanley Cavell, *Contesting Tears: The Hollywood Melodrama of the Unknown Woman* (Chicago: University of Chicago Press, 1996), p. 141.

14 The words are those of South Carolina plantation owner George Ogilvie as quoted in Philip P. Morgan, *Slave Counterpoint: Black Culture in the Eighteenth-Century Chesapeake and Lowcountry* (Chapel Hill: University of North Carolina Press, 1999), p. 100.

15 Brooks, *Melodramatic Imagination*, p. 4.

16 Eugene Goodheart, *Desire and its Discontents* (New York: Columbia University Press, 1991), p. 109.

17 The English subtitle translates the father's words as, 'Grow into a lovely lady, Anju.'

18 Cavell, *Contesting Tears*, p. 122. Cavell claims the realisation in film of the 'courage to become the one you are' is the source of film's power of metamorphosis or transfiguration, which is the nature of the medium itself and the source of its glamour.

19 Ibid., p. 5.

20 Ibid., p. 127.

21 The films Cavell identifies in the genre are: Ophuls's *Letter from an Unknown Woman* (1948), Cukor's *Gaslight* (1944), Irving Rapper's *Now, Voyager* (1942) and King Vidor's *Stella Dallas* (1937).

22 Cavell, *Contesting Tears*, p. 72.

23 Ibid.

24 Katô Shûichi, *A History of Japanese Literature: The First Thousand Years*, trans. David Chibbett (London: Macmillan Press, 1979), p. 1.

25 Cavell, *Contesting Tears*, p. 72.

26 For a full discussion of the noble exile see Norma Field, *The Splendor of Longing in the Tale of Genji* (Princeton: Princeton University Press, 1987), pp. 33–45.

27 Tobin, 'Le bruit des vagues', p. 32.

28 'Mizoguchi the Master', catalogue edited by Gerald O'Grady for the retrospective organised by James Quandt, Cinematheque Ontario, 1998, under the patronage of the Japan Foundation.

29 I would like to thank Chiharu Mukudai for her invaluable help locating and explaining Japanese material that was obscure to me.

30 Philip Lopate, '*The Thin Red Line*', *New York Times*, 25 January 1999.

31 Pierre Marcabru, in *Combat*, 7 October 1960.

32 The Heian era is known for its refined court civilisation. Mizoguchi represents the brutal conditions of popular life in this period, however. One English version mistranslates the epigraph: 'the origin of this legend goes back to a time when Japan had not yet emerged from the dark ages', and another 'this tale goes back to a time before Japan was civilised'.

33 Shunsuke Tsurumi, *A Cultural History of Postwar Japan* (London: KPI, 1987), p. 12.

34 Gilles Deleuze, *Negotiations*, trans. Martin Joughin (New York: Columbia University Press, 1995), pp. 125–6.

35 Yanagita would return briefly to the Sanshô legend twenty years later in a note in a literary encyclopaedia *Nihon Bungaku Daijiten* Vol. 2 [Japan Literature Dictionary] (Tokyo: Shincho-sha, 1932–5).

36 *Sanshô Dayû* was prepared in the summer of 1953; outdoor shots were taken in November and December, while studio work was completed in January 1954. The film was edited in February with final post-production in early March before its premiere late that month. 'Sansho' does not appear to be a subject that Mizoguchi had worked up long in advance.

37 Marilyn Ivy, *Discourses of the Vanishing: Modernity, Phantasm, Japan* (Chicago: University of Chicago Press, 1995).

38 See *Dai Nihon Hyakka Jiten (Encyclopaedia Japonica)* I (Tokyo: Shogaku kan, 1972), pp. 600–1 as well as *Heibon sha Dai Hyakka Jiten* I (Tokyo: Heibon sha, 1984), p. 495. The most distant extant version can be found in *Sekkyo Shu* (Tokyo: Shincho-sha, 1977). Among the few books devoted to this tale, see Iwasaki Takeo, *Sanshô Dayû ko* (Tokyo: Heibon sha, 1973–8).

39 Thomas Rimer, *Mori Ôgai* (Boston: Twayne, 1975), p. 107.

40 Antonio Santos, *Kenji Mizoguchi* (Madrid: Ediciones Cátedra, 1993), pp. 312–15.

41 An early Japanese review scorned as sentimental Mizoguchi's decision to invert the birth order of the children. Ôgai, the Confucian, maintained Anju as the elder.

Mizoguchi, obliged by the producer Nagata to give the Zushiô role to the already middle-aged Hanayagi Yoshiaki, decided to capitalise on the vulnerability of a younger Kyoko Kagawa whom he wanted for Anju. This reversal constituted the most serious impediment to the film's success in Japan, for it upsets the traditional chain of responsibility. To any Japanese, it is quite unthinkable that a younger sibling should facilitate the escape of the elder. It is the elder's job to be protector.

42 Santos, *Kenji Mizoguchi*, pp. 316–17, likens the mother's cry to a lingering perfume, a trigger of nostalgia that her children can sense preternaturally. But see especially the chapter entitled 'Tamaki's Cry' in Michel Chion's *The Voice in Cinema*, trans. Claudia Gorbman (New York: Columbia University Press, 1999). Chion claims, and does much to prove, that the mother's voice completely envelops the film with its spiritual significance.

43 Hirohisa Hasegawa has been responsible lately for theatrical versions of 'Sanshô Dayû', including a January 1993 production with the Acting Company Mito as well as a two-act opera staged on 29 March 1996.

44 Monuments for Anju and Zushiô exist in the Naoe-tsu. An elaborate monument, 'Anju zuka' containing a Jizô statue, can be found at Yura. An advertisement on the internet for an *onsen* near Maizura promises visits to the site of the mansion of Sanshô dayû. The 'White sand and blue-green pine trees' of the nearby Yurahama beach are an attraction that reminds tourists of the setting of this tale. Also, see *Heibonsha Dai Hyakka Jiten* I p. 695.

45 Marcabru, *Combat*, and Jean Douchet, *Arts*, 12 October 1960.

46 The umbrella in the illustration of the wandering Buddhist preacher symbolises the authority and ultimate shelter of the temple. See *Sekkyo shu*, pp. 396–9.

47 Mori Ôgai, 'Sanshô Dayû', in Dilworth and Rimer (eds), *The Historical Fiction of Mori Ôgai*, p. 161.

48 This text is reproduced in the Appendix to the Criterion laser disc of *Sanshô the Bailiff*. Geisler/Roberdeau Productions are credited for research on the history of the tale.

49 As in the painting, *The Churchyard*, by Caspar David Friedrich (1825–30, Kunsthalle, Bremen).

50 The first 'Prix international de la paix' went to *La Dernière chance* (Leopold Lindtberg, Switzerland, shot in 1944 but released after the war).

51 Nicolo de Pierro in *Twenty Years of Cinema in Venice* (Rome: Edizione Dell'ateneo, 1953), p. xviii.

52 The few attempts to distribute Japanese films before the war failed. After the war, not a single film from Japan played in Paris until April 1951 when *Samurai Bandit* by Eisuko Takizawa was released there. Then came *Rashômon*, opening to great acclaim for a run that lasted months.

53 Kurosawa claims not to have seen the Welles film when he made *Rashômon*.

54 André Bazin,'On Kurosawa's *Living*', in J. Hillier (ed.), *Cahiers du Cinéma, the 1950s* (Cambridge: Harvard University Press, 1985), pp. 261–2.

55 Jacques Rivette, 'Mizoguchi Viewed from Here', in Hillier, *Cahiers du Cinéma*, p. 265.

56 Noël Burch, *To the Distant Observer* (Berkeley: University of California Press, 1977).

57 Rachel Shteir, 'The Elusive Playwright', *The Village Voice*, 11 January 1994, p. 84. See also, *Vanity Fair*, December 1998.

58 To further internationalise 'Sanshô', Malick conscripted avant-garde designer Ishioka Eiko (responsible for the look of Paul Schrader's *Mishima*), Robert Wilson's German sound designer Hans Peter Kuhn, and 'lighting wizard Jennifer Tipton' (Shteir, 'The Elusive Playwright', p. 86).

59 Keinosuke Nanbu, '*Chikamatsu Monogatari* o Maegutte', *Eiga Hyoron*, January 1955, pp. 19–21. One of the most extended early discussions of the film by a Japanese appeared first in Europe, when Masamura Yasuzo published *Profilo storico del cinema giapponese* in Rome in 1955. The next year Masumura burst onto the scene with his youth-oriented films, so antithetical to the late works of Mizoguchi.

60 Here Mizoguchi uncannily echoes themes Paul Ricoeur at this very moment was shaping into his famous book, *The Symbolism of Evil* (Boston: Beacon Press, 1967). Ricoeur locates three types of myth by which cultures come to terms with evil in their midst: the Orphic, the Adamic and the Tragic. *Sanshô Dayû* intones each myth.

61 An impassioned review after the film's Japanese premiere insisted that slavery was still practised in Japan, referring surely to prostitution. Mizoguchi's last film, *Akisen Chitai* (*Street of Shame*, 1956), helped suppress it.

62 Kenji Tonomura, 'Mizoguchi Kenji Kantoku no Sanshô Dayû: Daiei Kyoto no Setto o Tazunete' ('A Report from the *Sanshô Dayû* lot'), *Kinema Junpô* no. 84, February 1954.

63 Mori Ôgai, 'History as it is and History Ignored', in Dilworth and Rimer (eds) *The Historical Fiction of Mori Ôgai* , p. 182. Ôgai published this essay just a month after the story of 'Sanshô Dayû' itself.

64 This view was eloquently advanced by Diane Stevenson and Gilberto Perez in a conversation with the author at Sarah Lawrence College, February 1999.

65 D.T. Suzuki moved to New York in 1949 and for a decade was the Buddhist guru at Columbia University where Gary Snyder, Allen Ginsberg, Jack Kerouac and others in the beat generation adapted his ideas. See Rick Fields, *How the Swans Came to the Lake: A Narrative History of Buddhism in America* (Boulder: Shamala Press, 1981) pp. 195–224.

66 Jean-Luc Godard, 'Mizoguchi', in Tom Milne (ed.), *Godard on Godard* (New York: DaCapo, 1976), p. 70.

67 Lindsay Anderson, 'Two Inches off the Ground', *Sight and Sound*, vol. 27 no. 3 (Winter 1959).

68 Helen Westgeest, *Zen in the Fifties: Interaction between East and West* (Zwolle: Wanders Uitgevers, 1996), p. 109.

69 Ibid., p. 135.

70 Recall the suicide of Martin Decoud in Conrad's *Nostromo*. Tying gold ingots to his body he sunk without a trace in the seas just offshore of a South American capital in the midst of violent revolution.

71 Malraux, quoted in Jean-François Lyotard, *La Chambre sourde* (Paris: Gallilee, 1997), pp. 28–9.

72 See my 'Echoes of Art, the Distant Sounds of Orson Welles', in *Film in the Aura of Art* (Princeton: Princeton University Press, 1984).

CREDITS
· ·
Sanshô Dayû

Japan
1954

Production Company
Daiei, Kyoto
Producer
Nagata Masaichi
Planning
Tsuji Hisaichi
Production Manager
Hashimoto Masatsugu
Director
Mizoguchi Kenji
Assistant Director
Tanaka Tokuzô
Screenplay
Fuji Yahiro
Yoda Yoshikata
Based on the novel by Mori
Ôgai
Director of Photography
Miyagawa Kazuo
Assistant Photographer
Tanaka Shôzô
Lighting
Okamoto Ken'ichi
Lighting Assistant
Iwaki Yasuo
Editor
Miyata Mitsuzô
Art Directors
Itô Kisaku,
Nakajima Kôzaburô
Assistant Art Director
Naitô Akira
Set Decorator
Yamamoto Uichirô
Paintings
Ôta Tazaburô
**Architectural
Authenticity**
Fujiwara Giichi
Costumes
Yoshio Ueno,
Yoshima Shima
Make-up
Kobayashi Masanori
Hairstyles
Hanai Ritsu

Music
Hayasaka Fumio
Traditional Music
Kodera Kinschichi
Mochizuki Tamezô
Music Director
Mizoguchi Kisaku
Sound Recording
Ôtani Iwao
**Assistant Sound
Recording**
Emura Kyôichi
Fight Consultant
Miyauchi Shôhei

Cast
Tanaka Kinuyo
Tamaki, Lady Taira; later
'Nakagimi'
Hanayaki Yoshiaki
Zushiô, Tamaki's son; later
'Mutsu-Waka'
Kagawa Kyôko
Anju, Tamaki's daughter;
later 'Shinobu'
Shindô Eitarô
Sanshô the bailiff
Kôno Akitake
Tarô, Sanshô's son
Mitsuda Ken
Morozane Fujiwara
Okuni Kazukimi
Norimura, the judge
Shimizu Masao
Taira Masauji, governor of
Mutsu
Araki Shinobu
Sadayû, Masauji's bailiff
Nanbu Shôzô
Taira Masasue, Masauji's
uncle
Naniwa Chieko
Ubatake, Tamaki's family
nurse
Katô Masahiko
Zushiô as a boy
Fujiwara Naoki
Zushiô as a child

Enami Keiko
Anju as a child
Mori Kikue
Shinto priestess at Naoe
harbour
Shimizu Akira
slavedealer
Date Saburô
Kinpei, Sanshô's head guard
Miyake Bontarô
Kichiji, Sanshô's guard
Kosono Yôko
Kohagi, young slave
Tachibana Kimiko
Namiji, old slave
Sugai Ichirô
Nio, old slave who tries to
escape
Soma Yukiko
Kayano, slave
Koshiba Kanji
Kaikudo Naito, finance
minister's envoy
Azuma Ryônosuke
owner of brothel on Sado
Horikita Yukio
Jirô of Sado
Ôkuni Hachirô
Miyazaki Saburo
Kagawa Rôsuke
Donmô, priest of Nakayama
temple
Hayama Jun'nosuke
old priest
Tamachi Kazuyoshi
justice of the peace
Kikuno Akiyoshi
prison guard
Omi Teruko
new 'Nakagimi'
Kongo Reiko
Shiono
Fujikawa Jun
Kanamaru
Shibata Sôji
man on Sado
Ishiwara Sumao
litter bearer

Amano Ichirô
gatekeeper
Oki Tokio
man at Naoe harbour
Komatsu Midori
woman at harbour
Nakanishi Gôro
guard
Koyanagi Keiko
Maeda Kazuko
prostitutes
Ishikura Eiji
Shiga Akira
Osaki Shirô
farmers

11,070 feet
123 minutes
Black & White

Credits compiled by
Markku Salmi,
BFI Filmographic Unit

Sanshô Dayû is available
on BFI Video, cat. no.
BFIV032, price £15.99